THE BOOK OF
TRURO

Cornwall's City and Its People

CHRISTINE PARNELL

Christine Parnell

HALSGROVE

First published in Great Britain in 2004

British Library Cataloguing-in-Publication Data.
A CIP record for this title is available from the British Library.

ISBN 1 84114 329 4

HALSGROVE

Halsgrove House
Lower Moor Way
Tiverton, Devon EX16 6SS
Tel: 01884 243242
Fax: 01884 243325
email: sales@halsgrove.com
website: www.halsgrove.com

Printed and bound in Great Britain by CPI Bath.

CONTENTS

Acknowledgements

I would like to thank all those who have dipped into their family albums to find photographs for this book. Like other Cornish people, Truronians tend to do things 'drekkley', and many people have had to put other tasks aside in order to find the pictures without which this book would not have been possible. Some people have taken the trouble to write down their reminiscences and anecdotes and send them to me; others, like Arnold and Vi Hodge, have invited me round for the evening and regaled me with tea and stories. I thank them all:

John and Patricia Allam, Mr and Mrs Arnall, H. Barnicoat, Paddy Bradley, Fritz Braund, Geoff Carveth, John Colston, Jennifer Dunford, Mike Edwards, Dorothy Gundry, John Hancock, John Haswell, Arnold and Violet Hodge, Eric Irons, Winifred Kinsman, Betty Lanxon, Joan Launder, Peter Lidgey, Robert Mallett, Barbara Martin, Andy McNally, Janet Mitchell, Margaret Mitchell, Robert Moor, Clarice Mortensen Fowler, Patricia O'Flynn, Barbara Olds, Fred Paddy, David and Denise Parnell, Brian and Sylvia Pascoe, Christine (Collins) Penhaligon, Chrissie Penna, Terry Purches, Sheila Richardson, David Roberts, Diana Smith, Jon Summers, Joyce Teague, David Thomas, Marjorie Toy, Wilf and Gloria Tyack, Paul and Simon Vage, Freda Young.

Special thanks are due to my husband Peter who has helped enormously. In his capacity as Recorder of the Truro Old Cornwall Society he has also allowed me to use some of the society's photographs and data. I must also thank Diana Smith who has been so enthusiastic about this book; not only has she written a chapter herself, but she has also borrowed photographs from most of her friends and family and brought them to me. Eric Irons has spent a whole year researching the facts about the coming of the railway and although I know that this is his special interest and not a hardship to him, I certainly appreciate all the work he has done. Jon Summers bothered to write down what he especially remembered so that all I had to do was to copy it on to the computer, and Barbara Olds allowed me to borrow freely from her notes. Mike Edwards had the foresight to write down the workings of Lakes Pottery in 1993 before he forgot or misremembered any of it and allowed me to copy out all his work. Without these contributions the book might have become too much of a personalised view of Truro.

Thanks are also due to John and Kay McBride at Bosvigo Stores and Neil at Kenwyn Street Post Office for agreeing to place flyers for the book on their counters. Hopefully others will follow suit but at the time of writing with the flyers only just printed those are the stores advertising this book. If I have overlooked anyone please accept my apologies; I should hate to think that anyone who has helped has been left out.

Diana Smith

Christine Parnell

Eric Irons

4

INTRODUCTION

When I was first asked as the secretary of the Truro Old Cornwall Society if members would like to participate in writing this book, I took it to the committee who considered the idea. I was disappointed with their decision but I understood it. They said that they thought Truro was too large and had too many residents for such a book to be easily produced and that the city had so much history that we could only scratch the surface. As we were not a little village they said 'no'.

I decided that I would take the project on myself and if any interested people wanted to help then I would accept gratefully. This book is the result. Truro does have an interesting history and this has only been touched upon, in order to provide a building block for this story. The people and their memories mentioned here are the ones who came forward, many of them after reading an appeal for photographs and information which I made through Mrs Jo Elsome-Jones, who, despite losing her beloved husband in 2003 and not being well herself, still writes for *The Packet* and the *West Briton*. Consequently the good people in the book only represent a fraction of the population of Truro past and present.

It was interesting to note that some things are remembered by most people who were around at the time but there can easily be variations in their ideas as we all remember things differently and time can blur the edges of what one thinks of as a clear memory. The one thing that seems to have remained as a clear memory for all those present at the time is the bombing of the City Hospital. Within this volume there are several reminiscences of that event. One thing is certain, the people of Truro were outraged and saddened by the deaths that occurred. Another devastating event was the demise of the Red Lion, which was inevitable as soon as it was hit by a runaway lorry in 1967. Everyone remembers it and, just as when President Kennedy was shot, they know where they were and what they were doing, although strangely not many people seem to have witnessed the accident. Perhaps that is just as well as there might have been some casualties.

It has taken a year to compile this book and I believe that everyone who has contributed has enjoyed the experience. We acknowledge, however, that this is but a starting point and freely admit to the Old Cornwall Society that *The Book of Truro* merely scratches at the surface of our city's fascinating and complex past.

Christine Parnell
January 2004

The coronation of King George V in 1911 brought the citizens out into the sunshine all dressed in their best. The town and the buildings are bedecked with bunting and flags but the children look a bit serious!

Chapter 1

A Brief History

Truro, Cornwall's only city, is set in a valley, leading out of which are a number of steep roads and just one flat one – which takes the traveller to Malpas. A small hamlet set on an arm of the Truro River at the head of the Fal, Malpas is believed by some to be the 'Mal Pas' of the Tristan and Iseult legend. Whether any truth lies in this is not known. Nor can we be sure of the derivation of the name Truro; some believe that it stems from the three roads, but it could also mean 'three rivers'. The three rivers are the Kenwyn, the Allen, and the little Glasteinan, and it was between the Kenwyn and the Allen that the original settlement grew up marked by one of the many wayside crosses which were scattered throughout Cornwall, marking the tracks for wayfarers.

A modern view of Malpas looking out through the window at the Heron Inn which was once called the Park Hotel and belonged to the Park Estate.

Truro's cross helped to mark the way for those travellers who came from the River Gannel at Newquay to the River Fal at Truro on an old trade route. It was Richard de Lucy, a Norman knight, who granted Truro its first charter c.1153 and the town thrived in the shadow of the castle on the hill.

Dominican friars came to Truro in the middle of the thirteenth century and settled in one of the poorer areas of the town, today's Kenwyn Street. They were

The old cross, which was believed to stand in High Cross 700 years ago, was missing for many years. Because the burgage plots on old maps turned sharply at this point historians are convinced that it was to skirt the cross, and records tell us that as late as the 1700s the bull which was kept on the site of the castle (which was in ruins by 1200) was regularly ridden down the hill by the scavengers and tethered to an iron ring in the base of the cross for bull baiting.

prominent in the town until the Dissolution of the Monasteries and now all trace of their buildings has gone, just a few stones remaining in the museum along with the face of a monk carved in stone at the site of what might have been their cemetery.

Although the black death wreaked havoc in the town, killing about one-third of the inhabitants, by

During the Civil War Truro declared for the Royalists and at one point, in 1642, was home to the Royal Mint as Exeter, which had been the site of the mint, was in Parliamentarian hands at the time. In 1645 Charles I appointed his 15-year-old son, the Prince of Wales, as commander of the western army. It was in this capacity that the young Charles came to Truro for part of the winter.

Truro Grammar School was renowned for its instruction in the classics and many pupils who later became famous passed through its doors, among them Humphry Davy of Penzance, who invented, amongst other things, the miner's safety lamp and discovered nitrous oxide or 'laughing gas'. Another pupil was Henry Martyn, who was a missionary who translated the Bible into several languages, including Hindustani and Persian. Samuel Foote, who became an actor and dramatist, was born and bred in Truro and attended the school. In later years, when he had achieved fame and fortune on the London stage, he would visit his old school when in Truro and he had the habit of giving the boys the rest of the day off which was more popular with the pupils than it was with the masters. Unfortunately it was a case of easy come easy go and he regularly spent all his money only to find himself in debtor's prison. At one time his sentence coincided with one being served elsewhere by his mother, also a spendthrift. Goldsworthy Gurney, who was born near Padstow in 1793, was another ex-pupil and he later went on to invent limelight and the Bude Light, which was a method he used to illuminate part of Pall Mall and Waterloo Place in London in 1842. It was his inventions using electricity and his steam carriages which made it necessary for standard time to be introduced throughout the country so that timetables had some meaning.

Truro had a carpet factory that gave employment to many, including the disabled, although it was the men and boys who worked on the best carpets and therefore were able to earn more money whilst the women and girls worked on the less expensive designs and earned less. By the 1870s, the Furniss biscuit and sweet factory was established and regularly sent out tempting aromas across the town. The rise of Mr Furniss' company coincided with the building of the cathedral, where there were many hungry workers to patronise his shop. By this time the railway had also arrived in the town, although it was owned by different companies, and some parts were narrow gauge whilst others were broad gauge. Both the passengers and the staff needed to eat, nevertheless, and it was a hand cart belonging to John Cooper Furniss that was regularly pushed up Richmond Hill to stock the buffet.

The face of the monk which is thought to mark the site of the cemetery of the friars of the order of St Dominic. A hawthorn bush on the same site still survives, although a part of it was cut down when the British Telecom building was under construction. Legend has it that if the tree was cut down there would be retribution and people would die but as it was not completely destroyed all seems to be well! However, the author has spoken to several people who have worked in that building over the years and it seems that no one felt happy to be in the building alone on the night shift and at least one lady has been convinced that she has seen a ghost.

1350 a coinage hall had been built, in the wake of Truro becoming a stannary town in 1327. Over the years there were lean times as well as more prosperous ones, but as a stannary town Truro had the twice-yearly coinage to boost her economy as well as a large amount of trade from the many quays all along the river front so this was a bustling place. The presence of the coinage hall gave rise to several smelting works and the town must have been very full of smoke and grime. Before the coinage, one might have seen blocks of tin lying in the streets waiting to be assayed and all sorts of characters would be thronging the town – porters, buyers and sellers and also those who just came to enjoy the atmosphere, giving plenty of trade to the inns. Over the years the smelting declined and with it the twice-yearly coinages. Other businesses began to prosper.

A modern view of the end of Boscawen Street and Duke Street show the building which now stands on the site of the old coinage hall and which perpetuates the name. This building in the Tudor style was built as a bank and is unusual in having the 'vault' upstairs! The original coinage hall was built c.1350 and was the end structure in a row of buildings which ran through the centre of what is today Boscawen Street and was known as Middle Row.

High Cross pictured in 1988 – giving us a clear view of the building which was once the Assembly Rooms with the Wedgewood plaques adorning the front. Thalia, the muse of comedy and idyllic poetry, is on the circular plaque at the top and the others are believed to be Garrick and Handel.

For many years Truro also boasted its own pottery and Lakes exported their wares all over the world with their unique square stamp on the bottom of their terracotta pots and jugs.

Although Truro is the only city in Cornwall, the county town was in fact traditionally Bodmin, and it was of course here that the assizes were held.

However, the opening of the new law courts in Truro in 1981 and the fact that the County Hall is in Truro means that it has now become the administrative centre for the county. Inevitably changes occur and beautiful buildings have been lost but Truro has entered the twenty-first century still retaining her own special character and charm.

In 1983 the old cattle market site was cleared to make way for the new court buildings. This is a very historic part of town as it was the site of Truro's castle which existed during the civil war between Matilda and her cousin Stephen and was probably built on the site of an even older Celtic construction. The bungalows in the foreground are the modern version of the old almshouses which were endowed by Truro's benefactor, Henry Williams, the woollen draper who died in 1629.

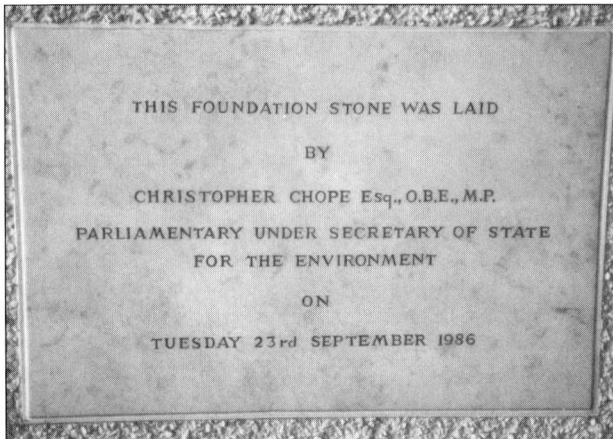

THIS FOUNDATION STONE WAS LAID

BY

CHRISTOPHER CHOPE Esq., O.B.E., M.P.

PARLIAMENTARY UNDER SECRETARY OF STATE
FOR THE ENVIRONMENT

ON

TUESDAY 23rd SEPTEMBER 1986

The foundation-stone of the Crown Court laid in 1986. Back in the days when the castle was situated on that site it was also the seat of justice.

The cathedral towers over the Red Lion Hotel, c.1950.

Chapter 2

✤

A Quick Tour of the Town

Boscawen Street lies at the centre of the city. It is a wide street because the row of buildings in the middle of the road, appropriately called Middle Row, was cleared away in the 1800s and nothing else was built there to take its place. In fact, for many years the horse-drawn taxis used to line up in the middle of the street waiting for hire. A wooden hut which was used as a room for the drivers was sited in Boscawen Street for many years although it has popped up all over the town at different times, most recently on The Green where it housed the car-park attendant before its eventual demise.

One of the most impressive edifices is that known as the Municipal Buildings, an Italianate-style construction designed by Christopher Eales in 1846. In the past the Municipal Buildings played host to the magistrates court that was situated in the Town Hall and for many years the police station was in the same building. The war memorial was erected in 1922 and at one time the fountain was close to it but this was moved to Victoria Gardens in 1937.

It was a sad occasion for all Truronians when a runaway lorry crashed through the front of the Red Lion Hotel having careered down Lemon Street and across Boscawen Street. The Red Lion had been the town house of the Foote family which was taken over as an inn in 1769. It was a beautiful building. Above the door was the date 1671 but when the building was being taken down and the staircase removed to Godolphin Manor near Helston it became obvious to the experts on site that what they were dealing with was actually an Elizabethan town house built in the sixteenth century. It seemed that all John Foote did was to build a new façade and perhaps make a few small alterations inside while the staircase was being built and he then had the current date placed over the front door. Most of the rooms facing on to Boscawen Street were Elizabethan. Although the supermarket on the same site has been built in a similar style it does not compare at all in quality or character!

Further along the street at the end of Cathedral Lane is the jeweller's shop, Samuels. This is No. 22

and the building was commissioned by Mr Ernest Huddy, a master jeweller who lived there with his wife Alice Maud who was a musician. The couple had a son, also called Ernest, born on 30 May 1903, and he was brought up in Truro and became a chorister in the cathedral. After studying music for a couple of years he decided to switch to medicine and became an epidemiologist. Dr Ernest Huddy who now lives in Dorset celebrated his 100th birthday in 2003. Mr Huddy sold out to Samuels who have been there ever since.

The building now called The Coinage Hall stands on the site of what was once the actual coinage hall where the tin was brought to be assayed; the pump outside the building also stands in roughly the same position as occupied by the old town pump. The poor old town pump is still working but is now in the public cemetery and has an ugly wooden box around. However, it is still used to draw water for the flowers on the graves. The coinage hall of today is in the Tudor style and is an attractive building with a pizza parlour on the ground floor and shops and Victorian-style tea rooms upstairs. By the time one has climbed all the stairs the tea is most welcome and one of the tables is situated in the bay window and has a marvellous view of Boscawen Street so is usually the first to be filled. On the way up the stairs is the 'vault', known as such because this building began life as a bank and rather than have a vault in the traditional place underground very close to the river it was positioned upstairs.

It was outside the coinage hall in 1789 that John Wesley last preached to the people of Truro. He came often and was in his eighties on his last visit when the town was in such a state with starving miners on the point of rioting that he stopped his coach and got out to preach. He was delighted that by doing so he could speak to far more people than could ever squeeze inside a 'preaching house'.

From the upstairs window in the coinage hall it is possible to look right down through Boscawen Street to St Nicholas Street and to Victoria Square. St

An aerial view of the town in 1985 shows, from top left, St Paul's Church, the police station, Radio Cornwall at Phoenix Wharf, the river flowing under Morlaix Avenue (the modern version of Boscawen Bridge) and Walsingham Place on the lower right side. To the left of the cathedral are the old Cathedral School buildings, Truro Methodist Church and the library and to the right is the coinage hall.

The war memorial was erected in 1922 so this photograph dates from soon after that date. Boscawen Street was always wider than usual for a front street since the old buildings of Middle Row had come down so there was plenty of room for a row of taxis to ply for hire by queueing up in the middle of the street. An ancient lorry turns to go up Lower Lemon Street, a manoeuvre that would cause chaos in the traffic layout of today.

The back of the Municipal Buildings was shabby before the Hall for Cornwall arrived but it has been turned into a very smart entrance to the theatre, restaurant and café. Rooms can be hired for private functions and when not in use as a theatre the seating can fold away and make room for fairs and flea markets.

A record of the building work going on at the back of the Municipal Buildings before its transformation into the Hall for Cornwall. The fly tower is shown under construction behind the Woolworths building. The building occupied by Woolworths has one of the few 1930s façades in Truro.

The Red Lion exterior is well known in photos but it is not so usual to see views of the inside. This picture of the oak staircase is interesting as the staircase itself can now be seen in Godolphin Manor near Helston. Fortunately it was saved when the building was demolished.

In July 1967 tragedy struck the town when the Red Lion was hit by a runaway lorry which careered out of control down Lemon Street gathering speed as it went. The damage was so devastating that the building had to be demolished. This photograph shows the driver of the lorry who was wearing a fire brigade helmet to protect himself while efforts were made to release him from the cab, not an easy thing to do as his left leg was trapped.

The main lounge of the Red Lion looked out over Boscawen Street. The inn also boasted a lounge bar and a cocktail bar and had 31 bedrooms, all with hot and cold water. The brochure tells us that it could accommodate 120 people in comfort. The beamed dining-room looked out over the hotel mews and St Mary's Street.

Boscawen Street, c.1910, is still recognisable today but a few changes have taken place. The horse trough has been moved farther down the street and now has flowers growing in it. The fountain (on the left) was moved to Victoria Gardens in 1937 where it plays on the lilies in the pond. The dining-rooms of Thomas James are on the left of the photo and so is London House looking as it used to before its makeover in the 1960s. Heard's Organ Factory on the right of the picture had organ pipes on the wall of the building as an advertising feature – this was next door to the printing works. The Red Lion with its lovely old lamp above the front door stands facing Lemon Street with its top-floor windows open for the air. Many Truronians would like it to be there still! Farther along is the old corn exchange building which was demolished when Littlewoods arrived. The taxis are waiting for hire down the middle of the road and all the little boys watch the camera. Where are the girls? Perhaps they had something more interesting to do!

A copy of a Robbie Johnson sketch depicting a scene in Truro in the eighteenth century, possibly on the site of London House (at the bottom of Lemon Street today). It may be one of Truro's old inns. The Bull (on the site of Woolworths) was one of the most famous and had named rooms such as Phoenix, Helmet, etc. Certainly the dormer windows set into slate roofs are a feature of Truro and some can be seen today in Princes Street.

Before cameras were commonplace, the sight of one would cause all manner of people to stand and pose even though that position had to be held for quite a while in order not to have a blurred image. Here people are dressed in their best clothes and the town is decked in bunting and flags for the coronation of King George V in 1911. Amos Jennings' grocery store was advertising tea at two shillings.

Another view of St Nicholas Street in the same era but on a work day. A taxi waits at the entrance to Victoria Place and in the foreground on the left the handles of a delivery boy's cart can be seen. At this time Mallett and Son occupy Nos 3 and 4 Victoria Place and Edwin Broad the drapers have a large store in St Nicholas Street.

Nicholas Street is named after the merchant's guild known as the Fraternity of St Nicholas. According to Charles Henderson, who was a great local historian, a deed dated 1278 referred to the guild as being the overlord of some of the houses in that road. No one seems to know when Victoria Place became Victoria Square; it was probably an accident on someone's part at some time that happened to stick. This is the site of the old West Bridge which forded the River Kenwyn in Truro's early days when the river's name was Dowr Ithy. It was also the site of the town mill that was powered by a leat called Tregear Water. Truronians are still very much aware of the water in this area of town as until recent flood measures were

put in place it was a regular thing to hear the old air-raid siren wind its way up the scale to a piercing whine and to find the river on top of River Street and Victoria Square, not under them.

One of Truro's best decorated areas at Christmas has always been Victoria Square and 1960 was no exception with each shop having a small illuminated Christmas tree attached to the first floor of the building as well as the lights criss-crossing the square. On the left is the Victoria Inn and farther along is the Galleon Restaurant with the postbox between them. In those days it was in the road but today it has been moved to the inside of the pavement.

The square leads into Kenwyn Street and it was here that the Dominican monks settled when they first came to Truro in the mid-1200s. They built their friary in the triangle of land between the river, Kenwyn Street as we know it today and St Dominic Street, although their land might have stretched farther up Chapel Hill in the direction of the leper colony.

The other street leading out of Victoria Square is River Street and to accommodate its building, the course of the River Kenwyn was altered. Three local families were instrumental in the development of River Street, the Ferris family, the Turner family and the Plummers. Ferris Town was built around the same time and named after John Ferris. Philip Sambell, the deaf mute architect who was born in Devonport and brought to Truro at an early age, was commissioned to design several buildings in Truro and he has left his mark on River Street with the museum (built as a savings bank in 1845) and the old Baptist Chapel built in 1848–50 and now part of the museum.

At the end of River Street it is possible to turn right and look up to the site of the castle once held by the man who did much to bring Truro into existence, Richard de Lucy. The castle came into his hands in 1140 although it is very likely that a castle, possibly an old Celtic fort, had existed there long before his time. Beyond the site of the castle towards the River

Left: *Although this is a modern photograph looking down Kenwyn Street towards Victoria Square (as it is known today), this is a very old part of town. This is the area in which the friars settled and built their monastic buildings. There was a meadow on the left side of the street stretching down to the River Kenwyn known as Friary Meadow. Their cemetery would have been on the right of our picture roughly where the car can be seen.*

Victoria Square is on the site of the old West Bridge and the River Kenwyn used to be forded here in safety. Today River Street has been built over the top of the river but it likes to remind us of its existence now and then and Truro has had floods over the years. In 1988 it was flooded twice. June Smith, the manageress of Fox Travel, is seen here being rescued from an upper window by the fire brigade. At that time the travel company had the slogan, 'Can I arrange your travel for you?' so as the boat being used came from Malletts, Robert Mallett called across to her, 'Can I arrange your travel for you?'

A night-time picture of floods in Victoria Square, c.1950.

Left: *A view looking up River Street c.1900 shows us what the front of the Congregational Church looked like. This was later demolished to make way for the 1930s-style Rural District Council Offices and today shops stand on the site. Next to the church on the right is the Liberal Club with the Temperance Hotel (later the Imperial Hotel) opposite.*

Allen is Pydar Street, probably the oldest street in town. It is named for the old hundred or administrative area to which it led (or from which it came), the hundred of Pydar. It was the main road leading down to the settlement near the cross and was on the trade route which crossed the county from the Gannel to the Fal and was much used by pilgrims and tradesmen.

Henry Williams, a draper who made his fortune out of wool, endowed a hospital for ten poor people in 1631 which later became the almshouses which stood in Pydar Street until they were cleared away to make room for the Carrick District Council Offices in the 1970s. Even now the snug little bungalows which replaced them are just across the road and known as Williams Court.

Pydar Street comes down into High Cross where the old Celtic cross has been reinstated in its proper place. It is believed to have stood in its current position for over 700 years and it was still there in the beginning of the nineteenth century and had an iron ring attached to it which was used to tie up the bull for bull baiting. At some point it must have been removed because it is known that in the 1950s the

shaft of the cross was discovered by workmen digging a trench in St Nicholas Street; not realising what it was they left it there. Farther along in the trench the head of the cross was discovered and the curator of the museum was sent for. Mr Douch realised that it must be the cross which had stood for so many years in High Cross and it was removed from the hole in the road and placed beside the west door of the cathedral where it stayed for many years. As Mayor in the 1990s John Christie had it re-erected in its proper position on a new shaft.

To the left of the cathedral the path meanders down to the mill pool and on to the old medieval bridge, once known as the East Bridge and now simply as Old Bridge. The road to the right of the cathedral, St Mary's Street, leads past the turning to Old Bridge Street and on towards the new bridge and then on down Quay Street to what was once Boscawen Bridge (now lost in the road known as Morlaix Avenue) and so we come to the river. This was the reason why Truro grew up where it did and the reason for its importance since the old port of Tregony, upriver, became so silted up that it lost its easy access to the sea.

For many years Truro had an unusual Post Office in High Cross which was designed by Silvanus Trevail and stood on its corner site looking down King Street. Inside it had many corridors and small rooms and it was eventually knocked down in favour of the building that stands in High Cross now, adjacent to the original site. When work was under way on the old Post Office plot to build Truro's first Marks and Spencer store, the new Post Office was revealed looking less than perfect! The Methodist Church designed by Phillip Sambell is on the left of the picture.

Left: A view from 1912 looking up St Mary's Street to the cathedral which was completed in 1910. The road was paved with wooden setts so that the noise of carriage wheels would not interrupt the services going on inside. Later the setts were covered over with tarmac as they became very slippery when wet.

Above: Truro is set in a valley with the river playing a prominent part in its rise to prosperity. This view c.1960 shows the river running up to Back Quay although large ships cannot come up this far these days. The Palace buildings which once housed the public rooms and the Palace Cinema are on the right. At the left of the buildings is Bishop Philpott's Library which once contained many specialist works for the clergy which have since been moved to Diocesan House at Kenwyn. On the far left is the Dolphin Buttery, a little café which used to be the Fighting Cocks Inn where Richard and John Lander were born. They both achieved fame for their exploration of the River Niger and are commemorated by a statue of Richard at the top of Lemon Street.

Below: Taken c.1958 from Treyew Road, this photograph clearly shows how Truro sits in a valley with the cathedral in the heart of the town. On the far right is the City Hospital which at the present time is closed and ready for re-development. Above the hospital chimney (which struck terror into the hearts of local children who believed that this was how amputated limbs were disposed of) is St Paul's Church with the teacher-training college (now demolished) on its left.

Chapter 3

The Port of Truro

by Diana Smith

Hidden under the streets of Truro run the rivers that were once bustling with the life of a busy port. The town of Truro grew up around its various trading routes connecting all parts of the county and linking to the world beyond. The land trading routes ran east via Grampound and Lostwithiel, west via Penryn and Helston, and north to the River Gannel and Newquay. The poor conditions of the roads accounted for the greater use of water transport and in 1205 Truro was registered as a port capable of accepting foreign commerce. Inland ports were common at this time as there was an ever-present threat of piracy and invasion.

The Festival of Light for 2003 had as its theme the river and therefore many of the lanterns represented fish and all things 'watery'. The mermaid seen here in Little Castle Street was carefully carried around the town and is now housed in the new Lemon Street Market where she is suspended above the shoppers with some of the other lanterns.

The routes of the Kenwyn and Allen provide us with an excellent starting point for navigating the layers of Truro's history and that of the important industrial port that lay at its heart. What would we have seen starting here on the new Piazza on Lemon Quay, for example? Beneath lies the River Kenwyn, once known as the Dower Ithy or Fragrant River. (It does seem highly doubtful, however, that the river

was ever very fragrant, bearing in mind all the town garbage and the offal from Mr Ferris' tanyard which might have been found in the leats flowing into it.) Lemon Quay emerged from an area of moorland known as Roper's Moor. As trade increased, Merchants Quay was built, and all along the banks of the Kenwyn industrial sites sprang up. A pottery, ironworks and many warehouses replaced the empty muddy banks. Imported timber was brought into Mr Sambell's timber yard in Fairmantle Street. He was the father of Philip Sambell, a deaf-mute architect, whose fine buildings still grace Truro today.

A ropewalk along the quay saw the manufacture of ropes required for the various ships that visited the port.

The Green attached to the original quay, Town Quay, was once subject to flooding, so over the years ramparts were built and eventually the area was filled in. It became a site used for fairs and other social gatherings. The Fighting Cocks Inn was then situated here and was the home of two of Truro's famous sons – the explorers Richard and John Lander.

Along Back Quay in the late 1700s was the fish market which dealt with one of the main exports – pilchards. Truro merchants involved in this industry included Francis Nosworthy and Edward Grosse. It was Mr Grosse who applied for a licence to import 1,000lbs of salt to preserve the fish.

So we see a wide river complete with all the signs of a busy port – ships moored along the quays and various industries being carried out to deal with all the trading requirements linked with the import and export of a variety of goods.

The River Kenwyn was bridged in 1798 for the provision of an easier access route into Truro. The building of a new road, Lemon Street, started the following year. This enabled the mail coach 'Quicksilver' a safer route into the town to change horses at the coaching inn Pearces Hotel (now the Royal Hotel). The mail was brought into Falmouth on the packet ships and then transported to London.

This fascinating photo dates from c.1900 and shows us much of the Truro of those days. The river comes right up into the town, and Lemon Bridge which covered the exit of the Kenwyn can be clearly seen. The customs house called Green House faces downriver and a ship is anchored nearby at the quay. The cathedral has as yet no towers and behind it and to the right is Brunel's old railway viaduct.

Back Quay (left) and Lemon Quay, c.1900. Truro had many quays and they were all regularly in use both for trade and pleasure. Garras Wharf and Town Quay were close by, and tucked around the corner on the left (not in view) was Green House where all dues were to be paid.

Into Robert's Ope and we see the Kenwyn under the bridge and along the back of the shopping area. Scavengers had the job of controlling the sluice gate under the bridge to let out all the waste from the town. On one occasion they inadvertently opened it up at the wrong time and the rush of water sent a fishing boat downriver from its moorings at Lemon Quay.

Continuing out into Boscawen Street down to Victoria Square and then Walsingham Place, ships would have been able to come up the river to this area, once known as Carribee or Cribby Island. A toll-gate from Malletts to a middle row of houses in Victoria Square spanned the old West Bridge, one of the two original routes into Truro. Here the toll-keepers collected monies for the upkeep of the road. Middle Row was eventually lost to a fire – was it because the fire engine came at a 'snail's gallop'?

The Kenwyn now continues under River Street and into the lower end of Castle Street. Turning into the Leats we see one of several channels created to power industries in the area, including the Town Mill at Victoria Square. Along the Leats we can see the steps where housemaids collected water for the families in the large houses nearby. The whole of this area from Victoria Square to Waterfall Gardens was once a Dominican friary.

Retracing our steps we come to Boscawen Street in the centre of Truro. This area became highly fashionable with mine owners building their town houses in the main street. Tin and then later copper from the mines brought increasing prosperity to the area. The coinage hall was the setting for the twice-yearly visits from the receiver and assayer to assess the quality of the tin and set the level of tax payable. From the early-fourteenth century this process took place prior to the export of the ore from the port.

Opes provided access between the two rivers and going along one of them we gain access to St Mary's Street – 'Squeezeguts Alley' – by breathing in you can just make it!

Now we move on to the northern side of the cathedral and the mill-pool – this is part of the River Allen once known as the Magna Aqua de Triveru Bighan – the Great Water of Little Truro. The mill-pool was once a large expanse of water and it powered the Manorial Mill. Further upstream at Moresk, once the tidal limit of the river, was the Duchy Mill.

Moving along to Old Bridge Street we come to the second river crossing into Truro, the old East Bridge. Ships of up to 60 tons came up as far as the bridge, which gives some idea of the size of the waterway that existed then. A new bridge was built a little further downstream in 1771 as the access into the old

eastern route was poor and resulted in many carriage accidents.

Along the banks of the river between the bridges we would have seen warehouses and quays. Many traders had premises in the area and these included Sweetland, Tuttle and Co. (with a copper-smelting business), Mr Rowe the bootmaker, and R. and J. Keen the coach builders.

Tin for coinage came into the town on horses and mules. Lines of pack animals, which could be seen alongside the quays, moved goods to and from the port. Tin, copper and pilchards were the main exports but a great variety of other goods were imported to supply various industries in the area, the main imports being timber for use in the mines and coal to power the smelting works. Other imports included skins and some buffalo hides for Richard Ferris the tanner, wool and dyes for John Isbell's carpet factory, and boiler-plates, pots, stoves and cylinder pumps for the mine agent John Moyle. In the 1660s included in the list of imports were French and Spanish wines, a bag of liquorice, 2 tons of iron, 3 cauldrons of coal, 14 barrels of tar and pitch, 2 sacks of wood, 12 bags of hops, a cask of aquavita, malt, a butt of currants, 6 barrels of grocery ware and a truss of cotton.

Taking the River Walk off New Bridge Street we come to Enys Quay and Furniss Island. Here the River Allen forks into two streams around what would have been a gravel bank and later became Furniss Island.

Imagine Avery's Creek where the Trafalgar Roundabout is today with the small River Tinney flowing into the Allen. The original gravel bank was linked to the creek by a small river crossing – Staddon Bridge, also known as Pons Glastennan or Glasteinen until 1823.

Samuel Enys, a wealthy mine owner, built his house and quay in this area. He would have been able to watch his tin and copper being loaded onto ships for export and timber being brought in for use in the mines on his own quay from his home at the Old Mansion House. He also built offices, a laundry and a cockpit in the area.

As the Allen gradually silted up over the years and with the increase in road traffic, it was decided to build another bridge over the river in 1848. Small ships could still go up into the quays due to the curved wooden structure on top of the stone piers of the new bridge. With continual river silting and decreased usage of the quays, a five-arch stone bridge replaced the wooden structure 14 years later.

Early tourism in the 1840s saw the use of pleasure craft plying between Truro and Falmouth. At first

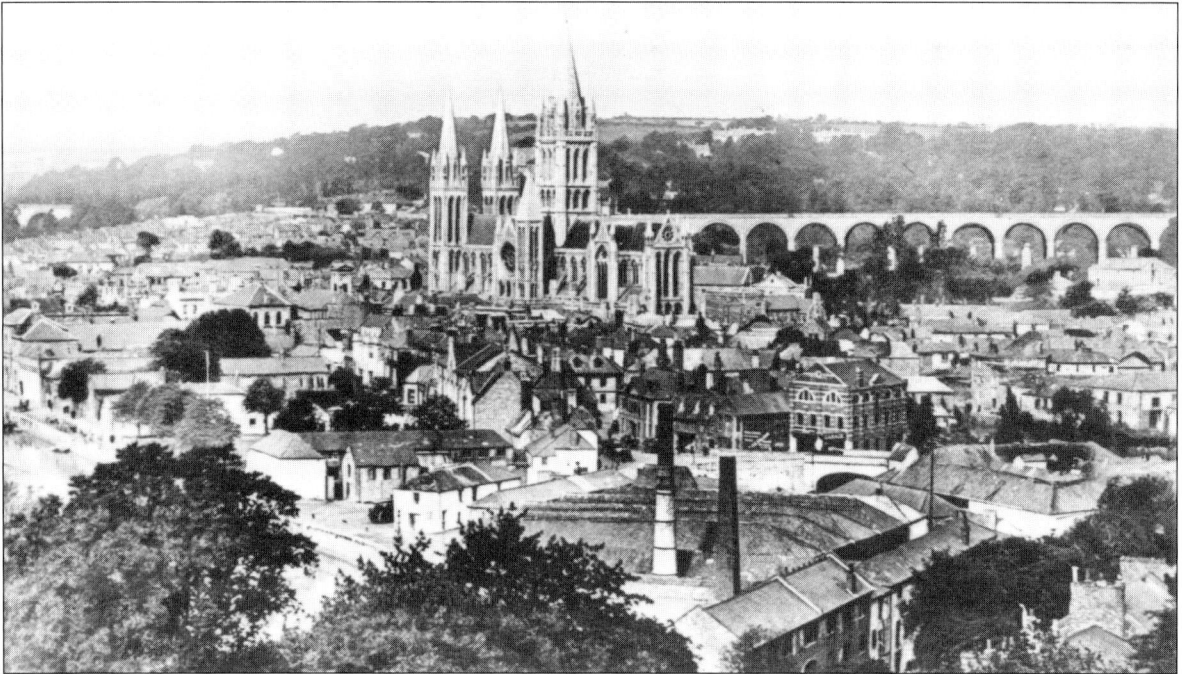

A general view of Truro c.1920 shows a completed cathedral and the stone viaduct which replaced Brunel's wooden construction. The river flows right up into the town and a boat is moored at Back Quay outside the Municipal Buildings.

Work in River Street in 1972 shows the arches which channel the Kenwyn under the street and down towards the Truro River. When River Street was built the course of the Kenwyn was altered to accommodate it.

As it was possible to get quite large ships up the river into the city until Morlaix Avenue was built in the 1960s, it was not unusual to see a ship moored close to town. On the right is the old gasworks, built in the early 1800s, and in this photo in the process of being demolished in 1955 when the new gasworks was built at Newham. Truro was one of the first places in the country to have gas and it was in use in the streets by the 1820s. The works at Newham did not last long as North Sea Gas made the gasworks obsolete.

The Old Mansion House was built as the home of Samuel Enys and he had his own private quay behind the house from which to carry on his business.

Town Quay was used for the passengers taking the river trips but as it was a trading area a new quay was built in 1910. This was Worth's Quay, reached by the underpass from Furniss Island, and it became the base for river trips as it still is today.

In the early 1900s Benney and Co. merged with W.J. Thomas to become the Falmouth Steamship Company. The fares were one shilling return, 9d. single and children 6d. One wonders if this included the little surcharge added on to raise money for the cathedral. It was Mrs Benney who gave so generously during the early stages of the building of the cathedral. Her face is shown in one of the chapel windows as the face of Eunice the mother of Timothy (the window on the left in one of the three chapels behind the altar – the one on the left).

Across Boscawen Bridge is Town Quay situated between the Rivers Kenwyn and Allen and where all the shipping tolls were collected.

The Town Council became increasingly annoyed at all the quays and timber ponds springing up along the rivers from which no tolls were ever paid. They took one of the merchants, Mr Barnard, to court for setting up one of these timber ponds. Unfortunately they lost the case and the treasury came down firmly on the matter of their funding of the case, which involved the mortgaging of a property in High Cross. Looking back towards Quay Street we would have seen the cooperages where the barrels were made for the pilchard industry as well as for the china-clay and arsenic industries.

The next quay is now known as Garras Wharf. Before reclamation this was a large mud bank, then it became Andrews Wharf and the home of Harvey's Timber Yard. After a severe fire at the yard in the late 1800s Harvey's moved to Trafalgar Wharf and renamed it Phoenix Wharf. This is the home of Radio Cornwall today. This area of land was reclaimed by Edmund Turner who was the MP for Truro in the 1830s. The old warehouses of HTP (Hosken, Trevithick and Polkinghorn) which once supplied flour to the Furniss factory have since been converted to luxury homes.

All along this eastern bank of the river down to Sunny Corner were more warehouses and several quays. These included City Wharf, Waterloo Quay – just below Trennick Mill and which was used by the Trafalgar Smelting Company – and Miss Kemp's Quay at Sunny Corner.

The western bank was also lined with warehouses and quays. In 1852 the railway line linked Truro and Penzance and three years later the line extended to the new station at Newham. Goods could then be taken to Newham Quay for transport via the railways. The Trethellen Smelting Company was also based on this side of the river.

We are now seeing the trading area move further out from the centre of Truro as the Rivers Kenwyn and Allen continue to silt up.

Timber imported from Russia, Sweden and Norway was kept in ponds along the banks of the river. Many of the ships moored down at Woodbury and the timber was transported up to the quays on flat-bottomed boats called lighters.

There has also been some boat-building carried out along the river with many small ships being launched into the Truro River. These include William Withell's yard at Sunny Corner, Scoble and Davis at Malpas, and John Vivian's yard at Newham.

Smuggling was rife around the Cornish coast with its many coves and rivers providing cover for this 'private venturing'. The River Fal with its wooded banks and creeks provided such cover and often an escape route for the smugglers in their attempt to stay ahead of the revenue men. Many a smuggler brought in barrels of spirits to be hidden and then sold around the countryside. The *West Briton* often advertised boats for sale that had been impounded by the Revenue from the smugglers.

A rifle range near Boscawen Park had to be closed in the late 1800s due to the potential danger of a stray bullet hitting a ship loaded with dynamite. The dynamite was produced at Cligga Head, Perranporth, and transported on wagons drawn by steam engines to Truro and down through Boscawen Street to Dynamite Quay at Newham. Fortunately this dangerous practice ceased in the early 1900s.

Truro had lost the main Custom House in 1671 to Falmouth and was demoted to a creek and all customs and excise removed in 1882.

The town of Falmouth received its charter from Charles II and rapidly grew with the arrival of the Packet Service in 1688. It was the growth of Falmouth as well as the continual silting up of the rivers that saw a subsequent decline in the port, however, and the trading activities gradually moved further away from the centre of Truro.

Truro and Falmouth held a very lengthy dispute over the ownership and control of the River Fal. Truro had always controlled the river as far as Black Rock in Carrick Roads but after the Civil War Charles II gave control of half the river to Falmouth. This gave Truro control to Messack Point, St Just and Tarra Point, Mylor, and the ceremony of beating the bounds took place at regular intervals. The Mayor and corporation would be taken by boat then across to the other point to renew the rights, liberties and precincts of the Port of Truro. This ceremonial party

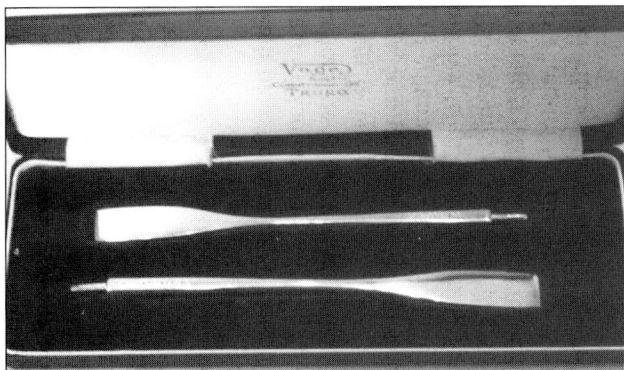

The silver oars which represent the authority of Truro over the river are presented to the incoming Mayor each year. They normally live in a Vage's jeweller's box in the Mayor's Parlour.

was often accompanied by the band who followed on in another boat.

The boundary dispute continued for many years and was the subject of many court cases. The Boundary Commission of Queen Anne in 1709 kept the status quo but the tale finally ends with the Admiralty High Court in the 1960s arriving at the same verdict.

The silting of the rivers continued to strangle trade links and several suggestions were mooted to try to deal with the problem. One suggestion was to employ the poor to remove the mud. Another idea was to deepen the existing navigational channel and provide another channel on the eastern side with subsidiary channels to the quays. The favourite must be the gentleman who dug up the mud to make bricks. All went well until the weather changed from being fine and dry to damp and the bricks returned to mud.

The weather often caused problems both within the town and on the river itself. Flooding regularly occurred in the nineteenth century and, indeed, up until recent times when flood-prevention measures were put in place. The West Bridge, The Green and Old Bridge Street were often under water. The patrons of the Barley Sheaf by the Old Bridge were said to be web-footed!

A tidal wave was reported in January 1880 and the following year the *West Briton* reported that the Truro River had frozen over from the Market House all the way to Malpas. Men in small boats went out with crowbars to break the ice so that shipping could move up and down the river again.

The centre of trading started in the heart of Truro and gradually over the years has moved further downriver. Eventually, in the 1970s, the port of Truro had a new base at Lighterage Quay. Mining ores were still exported from Truro up until the closure of Wheal Jane. The port has expanded with the

An aerial view of Lighterage Quay at Newham shows the Channel Foods fish-smoking factory and Lighterage Hill leading up to an industrial area of town.

purchase of adjoining property and land and with new storage facilities.

The port of Truro has seen many imports and exports throughout its history, but the most famous arrival by ship must be the organ for the cathedral, which arrived from London in 1887, and the Bath stone for the building of the Mansion House, which had come into Lemon Quay over 150 years earlier.

Truro today imports and exports a greater range of goods than any other port in Cornwall. Gone are the days of tin, copper and pilchards – nowadays it is cereal products, roadstone and scrap metal.

Port buildings on the waterfront of Truro in 2004.

Chapter 4

Local Shops

One of Truro's oldest family-run shops is Malletts. The company started in Fowey in 1880 and in 1892 they advertised in a publication called *Deakins Guide*, stating that they were 'furnishers and general ironmongers, saddlers, ships chandlers, plumbers and tinplate workers.' They also sold china and glass, sporting equipment (around 3s.6d. for a tennis racquet), beds and bedding (blankets started at 3s.0d.) and they were agents for life assurance. From 1904–11 the company also had a shop in Penryn.

The proprietor at the time of writing is Robert Mallett and it was his great-grandfather, Will, who started the business in Fowey then came to Truro in 1895 and opened in Nos 3–4 Victoria Place. In 1910 they leased 6 Victoria Place as well, then bought the freehold in 1921 for the princely sum of £1,800. There was a problem with No. 3, however, which was a constant source of worry – the river. The River Kenwyn flowed under the shop, in under the front door and out under the back door, and whenever the river flooded the shop floor was ruined and the stock damaged. Eventually the wooden arches which supported the shop floor rotted away and had to be replaced with iron girders.

It was in 1965 that Robert joined the company after learning his trade. He first went to work for Annears builders merchants at Penryn who, like Malletts, sold such items as sanitary ware, then he went to Holts, a traditional ironmongers in Southampton. Holts was run by an ex-Army captain with plenty of discipline for his staff and old-fashioned courtesy for his customers. Being courteous to the customers is something which Robert still expects from his own staff, whom he describes as 'like a family'.

When Robert started in Truro his father Denzil had steel stores at the back but Robert could see that being steel holders did not make them any money and he advised his father to get rid of the steel. His mother urged his father to 'listen to the boy' and the steel went. By 1967 Nos 3 and 4 had been sold and when the Moorfield car park (the first multi-storey in Cornwall) was being built in 1970 Robert bought a piece of land at the back of the store for £1,000 and built decking outwards to meet the car park. The decking and a staircase enabled people to enter the store straight from the car park and walk through to Victoria Place at the front. Later he placed a seat at the front and another at the rear of the store, one in memory of his father and the other in memory of his mother, so that shoppers could sit for a rest.

The Galleon Restaurant was put up for sale in 1988 and Robert went to the bank manager and asked

The unstable arch under No. 3 where the constant flowing of the River Kenwyn had weakened it.

One of the steel girders ready to be used to strengthen the old arch under Malletts shop.

Mallett and Son, The Galleon Restaurant, R.M. Smeath wine merchant and Avery Scales in Victoria Square, c.1960.

T. Mutton the butcher, P. Thomas and Son hairdresser and the Victoria fish and chip shop, c.1960.

Refrigeration and Engineering, Stewart Marriott and J. Summers with the Bristol and West Building Society above, all in Victoria Square c.1960.

GRAMS ...
IRONMONGER.

3, 4 & 6, VICTORIA PLACE,   Telephone Nº 50

TRURO. *Midsummer 1924*

Mrs. S. A. Chenoweth, Builders Cubert.

BOT OF MALLETT & SON,
LIMITED.
WHOLESALE & RETAIL FURNISHING IRONMONGERS,

HOT WATER & SANITARY ENGINEERS,
STOVE & GRATE MANUFACTURERS & BAR IRON MERCHANTS.

ALL ERRORS & DISCREPANCIES MUST BE ADVISED WITHIN 7 DAYS, OR NO ALLOWANCE CAN BE MADE AT SETTLEMENT.
ALL EMPTIES RETURNED MUST BE ADVISED.

This is an interesting bill-head from Mallett and Son with the date given as 'Midsummer 1924' and sent to Chenoweth, Builders at Cubert. One of the items was a coffin which cost £4.12s.6d.

The retirement of Mr Teague was celebrated with a presentation in the store. Mr Denzil Mallett with Mrs Mallett beside him hands a gift to Mr Teague who started work for them when he was 14 years of age and continued until he was 74!

to borrow enough money to buy it – this was over £1,000,000! He succeeded and the purchase went ahead. In the January of that year the river raised its ugly head again and flooded the premises, then it flooded again in October by which time Malletts owned it and the ground floor was ruined. The purchase of The Galleon had doubled the sales area and consequently more sales staff had been taken on. They all fitted in to the Malletts family atmosphere, so much so that during the October flood they all willingly stayed on well after closing time, without being asked, to clear up the mess and get the store ready for the next day's trade. By about 6.30p.m. Robert had realised the time and went out and bought something like 40 portions of fish and chips to feed the troops!

Three people from the staff of Malletts had a surprise when they were given gifts in appreciation of their loyalty to the store. The three of them had worked for Malletts for a total of 125 years! Ernest Teague had started as a boy of 14 and continued for 60 years, Ruby Cortis on the right had been serving the customers for 40 years and Edwina Hall had been there for 25 years.

Malletts shop, c.1950. Again it has a window display to attract attention and many people would have sighed for such equipment. The Galleon Restaurant is on the right and on the left is the lane which now leads to the multi-storey car park and the decking which Robert added when the car park was built so that customers could enter the store straight from the car park on the first floor.

The shop is still going strong at the time of writing and when W.J. Roberts and Son closed, Malletts took on their china and glass giftware department and also the linen department. Everything is now computerised

and yet history lingers on. The storeroom out at the back of the shop at the end of Walsingham Place is a very old building with echoes from another age and a history of its own. Walsingham Place belongs to the Enys Estates and none of it was ever to be sold, yet the storeroom has unexpectedly ended up in the Mallett family. Robert is not entirely sure of the facts but a family story suggests that his grandfather came by it as part of a bet, perhaps a card game! No one is sure, but Robert thinks that some money also changed hands, although certainly not the full value of the warehouse. Inside, it is surprising to find cob walls but with wooden panelling up to the level of a dado rail which, being in a listed building, cannot be removed. Apparently it was once owned by the Victoria Hotel and was used as a dance hall.

When Mr Denzil Mallett ran the shop, they sold coffins which were stored in the warehouse and one of his favourite stories involved a couple of ladies and their husbands, probably holiday-makers, who were walking past as some coffins were being removed from the warehouse and loaded onto a lorry. A look of horror crossed the ladies' faces as they saw the coffins and Mr Denzil thought he would play along. He rapped on one of the coffins and asked his workman, 'Who's in this one then?' whereupon one of the ladies almost fainted!

Like most other towns Truro's business community was made up of numerous family businesses in the past rather than all the nationwide companies that we have today. One such was S. Hicks & Son Ltd. Samuel Hicks the proprietor had bought a business in 1876 as a smith and coach builder in River

One of the things that Mallett and Son have always done is to attend the Royal Cornwall Show. This photograph shows their display for 1913 and Robert's great-grandfather William Mallett.

Roberts of Truro advertising their closing-down sale. In this photograph from April 2000 we see this store which had been a part of Truro for so many years selling off the stock. In 1904 a cow on its way to market wandered into the shop and startled the staff and customers alike and this event was commemorated 50 years later by a tableau in the shop showing a model cow and a horrified lady with her hands in the air trying to shoo it away. The store finally closed in June 2000.

Although this is a rather dark photograph, it gives us an insight into the ironmonger's store of the 1950s. This is Malletts when it was lit by large gas lamps and paraffin heaters were sold to heat a home economically. The moisture given out and the fumes were understood better later and their popularity as heaters waned. Most of the stock is contained in glass display cabinets or wooden boxes on shelves.

For many years S. Hicks and Son was a well known and respected firm. In 1876 Samuel Hicks took over the business at 10 River Street and he is seen here in the centre of the picture wearing the bowler hat. Although the writing on the back is not completely clear it is believed that it is William who is on his right and John who is on his left. The only girl is Millie. The family lived above the shop.

All Prices in this

CATALOGUE

except Wood Work,

are subject to a Discount of

°/₀

Private Address for Urgent Orders after Business Hours:

13, Cotehele Terrace,

Station Road, Truro.

Prompt attention given to
URGENT FUNERAL ORDERS.

Plates Engraved and Despatched
by first possible train.

Designs and Estimates submitted for

MEMORIAL BRASSES,

NAME PLATES, Etc., Etc.

In order to have a supply of coffins and furniture for all tastes and pockets, Mallett and Son had a catalogue of 'Coffin Furniture and Undertakers' Supplies'. The catalogue is full of illustrations of breast-plates, handles, brass nails, clips and wreath holders. Embossed swansdown side sets were priced from 2s.0d. to 20s.0d. and the price is even quoted for satin nail (for inside the coffin) and eucalyptus disinfectant.

Street. As well as shoeing horses he tackled any job that required metalwork, such as mending tools. By the 1890s he was selling bicycles and in 1900 he sold his first car. W.J. Burley tells us in his centenary book that it was Samuel's son, William, who went to Coventry to collect the car. Apparently the engineer from the car company, Humber, travelled back with William to teach him to drive and to help should any repairs be required! Hicks Garage became a well-known feature in Truro, trading from different places over the years, the last showroom being on Back Quay. The business ceased and the showroom was demolished in the latest redevelopment on the quay to form the new Piazza and the new Marks and Spencer Store.

Ashley Rowe, one-time recorder of the Truro Old Cornwall Society who used to write 'Chapters in the History of Truro' in the *West Briton* in the 1930s, tells us that 'Truro a century ago probably possessed a greater number of shops than at the present time.' It would seem that many shopkeepers were actually the makers of the things that they sold. For example, shoes were made in the town and it was reported in 1848 that on Wednesdays and Saturdays it was almost impossible to walk along King Street as the makers and vendors of shoes all had their stalls out obstructing the road which caused complaints to be made by members of the public. The shoemakers also went to neighbouring villages to sell their shoes and in 1834 a youth was charged with stealing 52 pairs of shoes at St Agnes market from a Truro shoe maker called Edward Jones.

In 1807 there was an interesting announcement made by S. Lawer who was not only a draper but also a grocer in Boscawen Street. He announced that he was taking 'this opportunity of informing his Friends and the Public that from 1 January 1808, he intend[ed] to confine the Grocery part of his Business to Ready Money.' In effect it was to be cash only for groceries but probably the drapery would be trading with people having fairly long credit.

Ashley Rowe also tells us that it was not unusual for a year's credit to be given to people of good standing and many of them who were in the tin business had an unusual way of paying. When they sent their tin to the smelters they received a 'tin bill' which they would then offer to the shopkeeper to pay their account. The shopkeeper would accept the tin bill, take his share of the money and give the change to the customer, therefore acting as a kind of banker.

One of the busiest trades was in the provision of stabling for horses which was all catered for by the inns of the town. The inns also provided restaurant services and rooms for hire for meetings – this was where the London newspapers were to be found. John Tippett advertised in 1811 that at the Eight Bells in Kenwyn Street he had, 'a London paper for the convenience of customers, three times a week.' Four years previously, in 1807, a bookseller who had a store in High Cross, H. Michell, advertised 'Books, Magazines, etc. procured from London every month.' This shows what improvements had taken place in the transport services in those few years.

To come more up to date to the 1950s, which many people can remember, shops and services were more as we know them now. West End Dairy was in Frances Street and advertised that they sold TT milk and could send cream by post. The proprietors were

Arthur Hamblin standing in the doorway of his shop in Pydar Street demonstrates that he is as tall as the door. The sign above his head says 'Beware ye mortals of these low portals.' Mr Hamblin was the Mayor of Truro, 1972–3.

FOR SOUVENIRS OF
TRURO & CORNWALL.

J. PEARSON & SON,
F.S.M.C.,

Watch and Clockmakers, Jewellers and
Qualified Opticians.

Splendid selection of Diamond, Engagement,
Wedding, and Keeper Rings.

SIGHT TESTING by a Fellow of the Worshipful Company of Spectacle Makers, London.

Repairs of all kinds promptly done.

17, BOSCAWEN ST., TRURO.
(NEXT CORN EXCHANGE)

Left: J. Pearson and Son were jewellers and opticians in Boscawen Street for many years. When Mr Pearson sold up to move to the bottom of Lemon Street it was because the Midland Bank wanted to expand their premises but in fact the lion's share of the extra space created went to Littlewoods which did not please him at all. Pearson's Ope is still a useful shortcut from Boscawen Street to St Mary's Street.

Right: An advertisement for J.T. Stephens and Son, c.1910.

J. T. Stephens & Son
GROCERS.

TEA, COFFEE & PROVISIONS of the Highest Class are offered on the VERY BEST TERMS.

OOOOOOO

ATTENTION
is called to the fact that we **roast** our COFFEE daily, and that our BACON is sliced by machinery.

Price List Free
on Application.

OOOOOOO

Telegram and Telephone Messages receive personal and immediate attention.

High-class Grocery & Provision Stores,
12, Boscawen St., TRURO.

TELEPHONE 93.

The West End Dairy in Frances Street, c.1960. Although the milk round and dairy products were the main fare on offer, the Venn family also sold fruit and vegetables and advertised the fact with a huge yellow plastic banana suspended in the shop window.

The Leats c.1955 was a very different place from that of today. It was forbidden to even ride a bicycle there and the park keeper patrolled the area making sure that people only walked. On the left is the footbridge across the leat to Mr and Mrs Lightbown's house. They were both musicians and Mrs Lightbown taught piano while one of Mr Lightbown's talents was as conductor for the choir at the People's Palace, the back entrance to which was farther down the road. Also along the road was the cottage home of Mr and Miss Weekes, where she sold Sunlight paraffin for lamps.

Mrs Fanny Venn and her son George but at the time that the author can remember it (c.1960) George and his wife Ethel did all the work. Ethel hailed from Jersey so her accent sounded very different to the local accents and unless one knew where she came from it was difficult to place her by her speech. In the days when the Venn family were remembered by Fred Paddy (known by many as a registrar of births, deaths and marriages), George kept his horse and milk float in the field in front of Richmond Terrace. He delivered milk to Chapel Hill, The Crescent, the railway station, Richmond Hill, Hendra, Comprigney Hill, Ferris Town, Edward Street and Castle Street. As well as dairy products they sold fruit and vegetables and often people had to choose whether they bought their vegetables from Venns or from Mrs Hammond who lived in Ferris Town (only a few steps away) and sold greengrocery from the room which should have been her front room. The Venn family 'worked like slaves' according to one local resident. They sold delicious ice-cream but often it was scooped out of the freezer and popped into the cornet straight after another customer had been served with some nice earthy potatoes which left the hands less than perfect – although this never seemed to do anyone any harm.

It was in 1902 that a new jeweller's shop was opened in New Bridge Street and Mr Vage was so successful that his family still run their own business from here (they celebrated their centenary in 2002).

From 1903 the founder, William A. Vage, had his sister Miss Mary Ellen 'Nellie' Vage working in the shop with him. She died in 1911 which was the same year that a smash-and-grab attack occurred at the shop. It is well known that before he could give chase to the felons Mr Vage had to stop to put on his top hat and tail coat as he could not go out improperly dressed. In 1913 Mr Vage decided to buy the shop which until that time he had rented and the next day he had a new shop front fitted, the same one that is there today. The unusual end to the theft story is that during the First World War Mr Vage's nephew was talking to a man in the trenches and realised that he was one of the men responsible for the attack. The firm celebrated their centenary with commemorative stationery and chocolates wrapped in gold for their customers. In 2003 they had chocolates wrapped in green with an inscription on the wrapper. The winner who deciphered the script won a diamond-studded gold cross.

Paul Vage remembers that when his father Donald ran the shop one of his customers was Guillaume Ormonde, the organist at the cathedral. He seemed to be a well-off gentleman and whenever he needed a

Paul and Simon Vage make sure that Uncle Albert is in the photo taken in their jeweller's shop in 2004. In nice weather Uncle Albert sits out in the sunshine with his Vage's carrier bag beside him.

Although it was the end of January 2004 when this picture was snapped, Uncle Albert's cousin Nicholas who had come to visit was still on the roof as getting him down involved some tricky moves. He has a clock peeping out of his sack (as if they didn't have enough clocks already, they are famous for them!).

gift for someone he went to see Donald. He would choose the item (the price was never mentioned) and that was it, he had nothing more to do with it. He would leave Vages to pack and send the gift and even to put a card in to say who it was from. At some time when it was convenient to him and when he had several presents to pay for he would go into the shop and say, 'I must owe you a lot of money Donald' and he would get his cheque book out and settle the account. He was well known for being extremely absent minded and on one of those occasions when he wanted to pay his bill he realised that he had forgotten his cheque book. 'Never mind,' he said, 'just give me some paper.' From a blank piece of paper he cut a cheque-shaped oblong, put a postage stamp on it and wrote his own cheque which was accepted by both Donald and the bank without a quibble.

An unusual thing about the shop is that set into the floor between two counters is a clock which must have been a challenge for the carpet layers. Simon Vage recalled that in the past they had a letter addressed to, 'The Jewellers with the Clock in the Floor, Truro' and it reached them without any difficulty or delay as the postman knew exactly which shop it was!

Farther down the road from Vages is the chandlery of Mark Langdon. Mark is the fourth generation to have the shop, although years ago it sold bicycles. Reg and John Langdon's shops are well remembered. One unusual thing about the shop in New Bridge Street is that part of the shop floor is tiled in the old wooden setts that used to abound in Truro. St Mary's Street was paved with them in order to cut down on the noise of horses and carriages which would disturb the services in the cathedral, although the road is covered in tarmac now as when wet the wood was extremely slippery. Mark does not know for sure where his setts come from but thinks it is possible that when New Bridge Street was re-surfaced, some of those setts were re-used. They certainly look very attractive with a coat of varnish.

One shop that many people remember with fondness was J. Summers and Son, an animal-feed shop. In those days people could walk through to cut off the corner – maybe buying some bird seed and scattering pigeons that pecked hopefully at the ground. Rowes the bakers occupy the same site now and the shop still has two doors, one on River Street and one on Victoria Square. Jon Summers has written a short account of the shop's history while it was in his family:

I've jotted down a few notes about our family's time at 'The Mill Stores' 22 Victoria Place. (Old notepaper headings show 'Place' not 'Square'.) My grandfather, John Summers, acquired the property around 1917. The family, two girls, Millicent and Margaret, and one boy, Norman (my father), moved into the accommodation over the shop premises. Previously the property

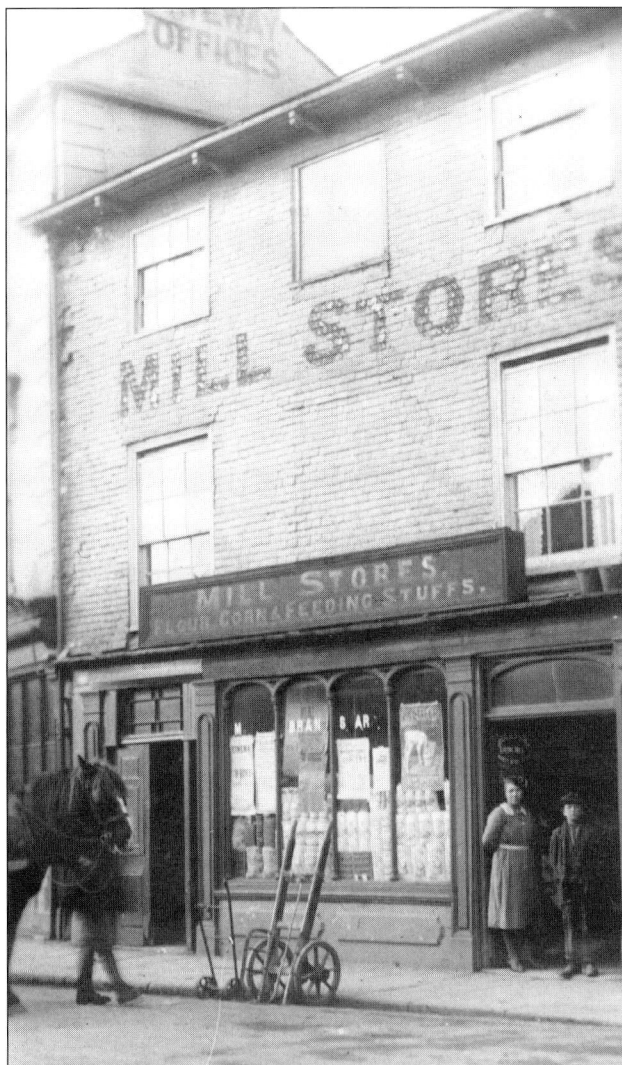

The Mill Stores in Victoria Place, c.1920. Jon Summers does not know who the people are in the doorway but would like to think that the girl is one of his aunts.

had been owned by the Carne family who, amongst other business interests in Truro and Falmouth, owned and operated the mill at Coosebean.

I have always understood that at this time Coosebean was an animal feed and flour mill but I believe it is often described as a paper mill. At the time 22 Victoria Place was acquired, my grandfather and family were living in the mill house at Coosebean. I have always assumed that the shop was the retail outlet for the mill at Coosebean.

It is interesting to note that prior to acquiring the shop, my grandfather was employed as the manager of the agricultural machinery department at the Edwards Brothers business situated on the site of the present Penrose Camping store on the quay.

A few years later changes were made to the premises and Roy Trevail started his gentlemen's outfitting business with an entrance in River Street. The business proved successful and my grandfather bought the house

in Edward Street known as Trecurra Lodge. This property was previously owned by Mr Ben Edwards who was, I believe, the owner of the business on the quay. I have always known the property as two houses, but as my grandfather owned both, it was no doubt originally one large town house.

Until the major floods in 1952, my grandfather was a familiar figure behind the old mahogany counter in front of which were the various hessian bags of dog biscuits and poultry feed. Many old Truronians will remember the wooden box behind the shop window containing mixed corn and beside that the platform scales.

In the early 1950s premises in Malpas Road were bought. These premises were owned by George Dixon and Son. Dixons were wholesale grocers and jam manufacturers, presumably using Kea plums brought up the river from Roundwood Quay by punt. Changes were made to the river side of the premises, machinery installed and for the next twenty years many cargoes of grain and animal feed were discharged from coasters coming mainly from France, Antwerp and Rotterdam. The Victoria Place shop ceased trading in around 1965 and Victoria Wharf (named after Victoria Square) closed down in 1969, so ending over fifty years' trading.

An interesting feature in the Victoria Wharf building was the place where Dixon's steam lorry was parked at night. This was on the ground floor of a two-storey building. In the floor and ceiling of the room above were two holes, one above the other, to allow the smoke from the vehicle's chimney to escape!

Mr Summers also said that the reason that his grandfather was not in the shop after the flood in 1952 was that it caused him to have a stroke and he later died. One thing that the author remembers about the shop was the smell of the corn and various seeds and how the sacks of seeds always had a scoop sitting on the grain ready to weigh it up in paper bags for the customers.

There were many local shops in the town about 50 years ago, too numerous to mention, but some names may revive memories: Greens the delicatessen, Corks sweet shop (two shops, one in King Street, the other in Frances Street), Mr Heddon's sweet shop in Kenwyn Street and Mr Davey the grocer – another of the little shops in Frances Street. Farther down towards the town was Lampier's, also grocers, Rickards the pram shop, Moons who sold pianos and sheet music and so on into the centre of town where the drapery of W.J. Roberts was a feature of the town.

For many years Hendra's pharmacy in Lower Lemon Street was one of our local firms but recently it has become one of the Moss chemist's shops;

Norman Summers some 20 years later leaving the shop. The rounded wall advertises hay and straw and a PDSA collecting box sits in the doorway.

Norman Summers when he was about 20 years old is looking after a horse outside his father's shop in Victoria Place.

The window of Bullen and Scott the ironmongers in Lower Lemon Street c.1930.

Rachel Dale (left) *and Michelle Reed are two of the waitresses in Charlotte's Tea Rooms which is situated upstairs in the building on the site of the old coinage hall. It is quite a climb up the stairs but worth it when you get there!*

however, the Hendra family still have a health-food shop and a gift shop next door to the pharmacy in Lower Lemon Street so people can still go to Hendra's as they 'belong to do'! One of Truro's new and attractive outlets is the refurbished Lemon Street Market for which the Hendras are responsible. For many years the market was a run-down building which had a number of retail outlets much frequented by the people in the know. It was possible to buy 'second day bread and cakes' there which was something appreciated by pensioners and those on a low income. Another shop had pet food, yet another was a barber's shop. What with the fruit and vegetables, the café, the second-hand shop and all the others many people were not happy when it closed its doors for refurbishment but what a transformation it has been! It has been made into a clean modern building but still retaining its one special feature, the turntable (built there when it was a mews) which was used many years ago to turn the carriages of the gentry so they could exit into Lemon Street. It still has an excellent selection of shops with a new addition, an upstairs area where there is a brand-new café and a marvellous selection of artwork including some famous names.

Over time the shops are bound to change, not only their ownership but also style of the façade and the type of goods to be sold. In recent years one could say that although the centre of the city is still Boscawen Street, many of the shoppers also made for the High Cross area. Today the Piazza and Lemon Quay draw people, perhaps because of the relocation of Marks and Spencer and the new shops appearing there. In the run up to Christmas 2003 a huge marquee was erected on the Piazza and filled with the stalls of businesses who had subscribed to the 'Made in Cornwall' scheme and everything from chocolate to candles, toys to artwork was on sale there. As Truro's shopping centre expands (and there seem to be ever more plans afoot) perhaps the hardy shoppers will have to do it in stages and visit different parts of the city on different days!

These ladies work in the building which once saw many glamorous occasions. Warrens Bakery is situated in High Cross in what was once the site of the Assembly Rooms and which fortunately still has the beautiful façade. From the left they are: Jan, Melanie, Sue, Michelle, Nikki and Jane. Once people gathered there for balls and theatre performances, these days they are looking for bakery products or perhaps a nice cup of coffee with a view of the cathedral and the goings on in High Cross.

T. Mutton & Son.
HIGH CLASS
BUTCHERS & GRAZIERS

'Phone 2028

Established over 60 years

Deliveries to all Parts Daily

Personal Supervision

PURVEYORS T. MUTTON & SON

VICTORIA SQUARE ··· TRURO.

Up-to-Date Refrigerators on the Premises
Purveyors of SUPER QUALITY ENGLISH MEAT

Muttons the butchers was on the corner of Victoria Place and Kenwyn Street for many years and usually caused amusement because the name was so appropriate to the occupation.

Mark Mitchell points to the coloured glassware in the window of the family firm, Truro Glass, in Tabernacle Street. Not only are they glaziers but they also have one floor of the building devoted to all styles of mirrors. They also deal in stained glass and many people have learnt to create their own works of art. The building is named after Truro's little river, the Glasteinan, which trickles down through Tregolls and is reputed to have been once full of clear sparkling water just like glass!

The old wooden setts, possibly from New Bridge Street, now varnished and forming an attractive floor in part of Langdon's shop.

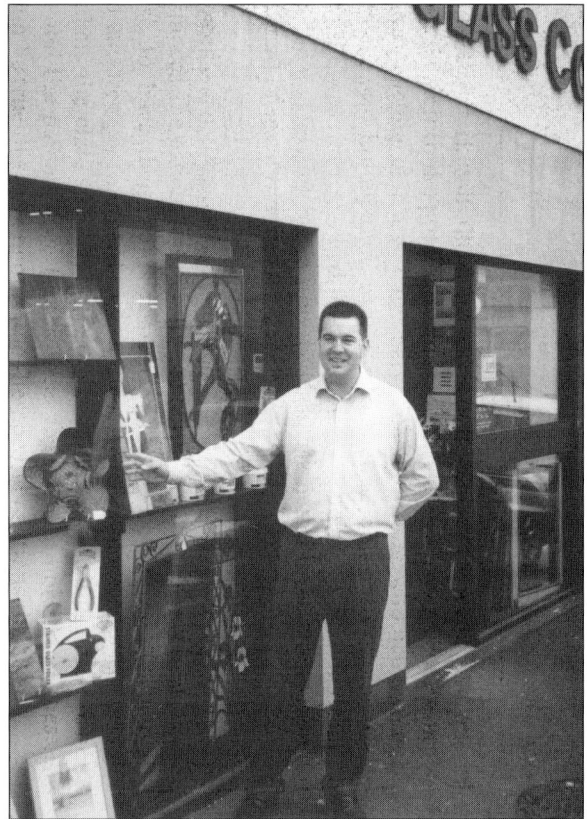

Mark Langdon is the fourth generation of his family to run the business in New Bridge Street, although many people will remember it for bicycles.

Chapter 5

Lakes Pottery

Barbara Olds has been interested in the pottery in Truro for many years and when her daughter Alison had a 'pocket-money job' there as a guide in the 1970s, Barbara started collecting little bits of information about the history of a pottery on the site in Chapel Hill.

In 1968, when the site was being excavated to make the base for the new electric kiln (and at which point there were just eight old-fashioned potteries left in Britain), the base of a far older kiln was discovered which was dated to 1670 by an archaeologist. In fact, it is believed that a pottery existed on the site even further back in time – as long ago as 1250! The potters here had for centuries been handcrafting their wares before mass production and they still used the same methods until very recently. All Britain's old potteries were situated close to the raw materials and, in the case of Truro, the clay was in the pottery yard, the material for making the glazes came from the heart of the town (and could still be found under the Littlewoods store in Boscawen Street in 1968), and the gorse for firing the kiln was to be found in abundance in the area around Truro.

As anyone who was taken on a tour of the pottery by Alison will remember, the site includes a cloam over. Cloam ovens were, in essence, large open fireplaces built into the wall at an angle to the fireplace which were filled with wood, lit, stoked and became white hot. The ash was raked out onto the open fireplace, the oven was mopped out with a rag on a stick, and meats, pies and bread were traditionally placed inside. The meats and bread were left for approximately an hour and a quarter to cook and if one had stoked correctly the residual heat would be just right for baking lighter items such as buns. The little door which one sees in front of the cloam oven at the pottery was placed in position with a rod stretching from the door to the floor to keep it in place.

After showing the customers items as they would have looked at various stages in the glazing and firing, Alison showed visitors a piece of 300-year-old pot which had been dug out of the wall of the 1670

kiln and they were able to compare it with a piece of the modern slipware and see how similar it was. She also showed them little jugs that had been made on the wheel by the potter and told them that the Queen Mother had had them twice for the royal children. Alison would then explain about the piggy banks:

The piggy banks are also entirely hand made and have been made here for over 90 years. As you see they have different expressions. They will take at least £5 worth of sixpenny bits and however large the mouth, the coins will not fall out!

Mike Edwards worked at Lakes Pottery for many years and after it had closed permanently he felt that he should write down everything that he could remember about the working practices and employees, and he has kindly agreed to his memories (1993) being included in this book.

Slurry and Knubs

Henry Venn's Pottery was situated on the then riverbank behind St. Clement Street approximately [at] the rear of Halford's building. Clay, mostly from Fremington, North Devon, was apparently brought in by a barge directly to the premises. The wares manufactured were all for domestic use, i.e. water pitchers, pans, plant pots, etc. The pottery gradually declined through the period of the 1914–18 war, probably through lack of manufacture and finally closed in the early 20s. The remaining staff including Mr Henry Venn, Mr Barry Pascoe and I believe Mr Bill Collins moved to the pottery in Chapel Hill, then being run on a much smaller scale and also run down, later to be known as Lakes Cornish Pottery. The proprietor, a Welshman, Mr Tucker, soon joined in partnership with Mr W.C. Lake who was at that time proprietor of a builder's merchants at East Hill, St. Austell. Production increased perceptibly during the 1920s. The original kiln was enlarged, more of which later. Some clay was used from the St. Agnes clay works but still mostly from North Devon, now being brought into Truro railway

Mike Edwards and his wife Stella enjoy a break in the sunshine outside the making shop in 1950.

sidings and transported to the pottery by horse and cart.

The very steep entrance road into the yard was cobbled, as was the yard and clay pit area. This was to give the horses added grip. In 1946 the yard and entry was tarred but the centre part of the access slope was left cobbled as a feature. Two horses were employed at the time, one to draw the cart and the four wheeled delivery wagon driven by Bill Collins. The other horse permanently powered the clay mill; harnessed to a long beam, he would amble round the circular cobbled track driving the pug mill, a large circular wooden barrel like device with rotating blades inside, geared at the top of the shaft and loaded with rough clay at the open top with a shovel. The clay would be forced downward under its own weight to emerge at a slot under the mill, in the shape of approximately half hundredweight blocks of clay named 'spits'. These blocks would drop onto a specially shaped shovel, the handle of which would rise when ready to remove it from the mill. It was said that the horse, a wily creature, would immediately stop walking around when he noticed the handle was up and could only be started again when a lump of clay was hurled at him by the 'boy' tending the mill!

The clay pit adjoining the mill was situated in a corner of the yard by Bosvigo Road, usually heaped up with clay to a height of around fifteen feet and holding upwards of twenty tons of clay at a time. This was 'topped up' continually by horse and cart from wagons

at Truro railway sidings up the road. This could be very heavy and hard work with a shovel as in wet weather the clay was exposed in the wagon in transit and would become waterlogged and difficult to handle. The yard man and a boy would 'pull down' from the pit a layer of raw clay, to a depth of about a foot, across the cobbled area in front of the pit. This layer then if a bit 'dry' would be dowsed with buckets of water from the hand pump at the well. If already wet it would be left alone for a couple of days then the batch would be 'cut' using a special square bladed long handled shovel with a downward twisting action in close rows of cuts across the batch and continuing until all the harder lumps were dispersed. This operation would take a day's work, the men being liberally caked with clay up to the knees! The following day the batch would be 'rounded up', that is built up by shovel into a large block resembling a huge loaf of bread. This block would be in the region of eight feet by five feet high and would contain around four tons of clay. This would then be covered with wet sacking and left for a couple of days while the next batch was 'pulled down' alongside. The block would then be moved into the mill building alongside the clay pit by means of one man cutting squares from the block with a wetted shovel, dropping his shovel full inside onto another man's shovel who would carry it across the cobbled floor of the mill and start to build another batch block adjacent to the horse track. Sometimes if the yard men caught up with the needs of 'makers', i.e. if the makers were making a lot of small ware and this was not using up so much clay, the batches around the mill would completely surround the track so tightly that the poor old horse would be 'lagged' all on one side with clay stuck to him as he brushed by the batches on his dreary task! At the end of the working day he would have to be dowsed with water from the well, and brushed down with a broom before being stabled for the night.

These batches of clay would be covered with sacking which would have to be kept wet to stop the clay from drying out, one batch in rotation would be uncovered and fed by shovel into the mill. This clay preparation was a continuous operation employing two men and a boy, very hard work, especially in winter conditions as it was imperative that frost was prevented from entering the clay. Batches were often covered with straw then dry sacking. There was no electricity connected to the premises until shortly before the 1939–45 war so all operations needing illumination had only candles, or at best a paraffin lantern. The well being the only water supply was actually a bonus in winter especially for the 'maker' as the early morning pitcher of water for the wheel was warm, stemming from deep underground. There was no heating in the maker's shop and the water left in the wheel box overnight had often turned to ice.

It had to be broken up before work could commence, so the warm water was most welcome.

A further word about the horses. During the summer months, both the wagon horse and the mill horse would be placed in a field at Redannick overnight where they no doubt revelled in their freedom, so much that the task of rounding them up before work each day was some job! The boy would be sent first, armed with a rope, only to return some time later, crestfallen and covered in mud with no horses, swearing and cursing saying "I can't catch un boss". Then after more cursing and swearing the whole staff would troop across the field for the daily round up before work could begin.

Back now to the clay preparation. The milled 'spits' were taken to the wheel shop next to the mill for further preparation for use on the maker's wheel. This task was usually allotted to the 'boy', hard and heavy work [it was] too, the spits weighing over half a hundredweight each, and difficult to handle. These would be deposited at the end of the wedger's bench. The wedger was of necessity a strong man. Wedging consisted of lifting one spit above head level and bringing it down with a resounding thump on to another one, then repeating the process and cutting across continually with a wire to test consistency and to remove any foreign bodies. Small stones, particularly limestones, were a constant problem. It was also the wedger's task to ensure that the 'stiffness' of the clay was correct for the needs of the wheel man, as very large items – chimney pots, etc. – could not be made with too hard a clay. Small jugs, etc. could, so the wedger would blend, possibly a very stiff split with a softer one, to get it right before 'balling up' the clay for the wheelman. No balls were ever weighed. The wedger and the wheelman would work out the quantities at the start of making, and woe betide the wedger if the wheelman found the balls to be too 'light' half way through filling a nine foot wareboard with pots! If the consistency was not just right, he would be told in no uncertain terms, "This 'ere is nawthen but slurry and knubs, my son."

The 'wheelman', never in those days referred to as a thrower, was in the pre-war years Mr. Henry Venn, whose own business had closed earlier. Henry was a large gentleman; he needed to be, as a lot of very large items were made by hand on the wheel in those days. Four-foot chimney pots [were] made in two halves and later 'run' together... as were flower pots up to eighteen inches across. Rhubarb and kale pots, made in one piece, were up to three feet high requiring two men to lift from the wheel. Nine foot long wareboards some twenty inches wide were used for these large items some of which had around twenty to thirty pounds of clay in their manufacture. A full board of ware could be around one and a half hundredweight causing two men to

The kiln at Lakes Pottery was a familiar landmark for many years. Writing about the closure of the pottery a Mr H.D. Clift wrote to the West Briton Argus (the Monday edition) in 1987 stating 'There don't seem to be many traditional things left in Truro, perhaps only the old Monday night West Briton and the City Hall.' Now they are all gone.

grunt if they had to carry it far! The freshly made boards of ware for the most part were carried back into the mill house behind the making shop, the area next to the kiln which was equipped with very strong wooden horizontal rails, on to which the full boards were mounted to start the drying process. Normally, the next day the clay would have dried sufficiently for any further work to be done. That is, the halves of the large chimney pots were put together back on the wheel, holes would be cut in the bases of the large plant pots, and the walls 'dressed' by rubbing the clay with the palm of the hand. Small stones would now be found and removed. Handles would be pulled or 'bawed' on to the pitchers and on to the sides of large cream pans. Rhubarb and kale pots would have been turned upside down and a section of the bases cut out. This work would normally have taken place back in the end part of the making shop or outside if the weather was good enough. Necessary work having been done, the boards would have been taken across the yard to the 'fire house' where they would be dried completely until required for firing. The glazing or 'metalling' would have been done in the making shop. Before final drying in those days red lead oxide would be used with an ingredient of slip, i.e. liquid clay. This glaze gave the famous 'trout back' finish to all the early Lakes pots. Red lead was eventually replaced by 'galena' (blue lead) oxide, which gave a glossy dark-brown finish. All pitchers and items which were intended to hold liquids were glazed inside only with lead glaze. Mr Barry Pascoe would carry out this operation and also became the 'wheelman' on Henry Venn's retirement at the beginning of the war.

A tremendous variety of items was produced from one and a half inch flower pots to the very large items previously described. The variety of output by the wheelman was governed I presume by demand at the time and what was held in stock. The kiln was fired monthly and a full load of thousands of items would be dried and ready for the kiln packing when needed. After each firing the boss, Mr Lake, would come and sit on a stool near the wheelman and brandishing a piece of paper would proceed as follows "Henry, better have four boards of twenty inch pans, one board of four foot pots, two board of kale pots, six boards of each size pitchers, ten boards of each size flower pots this time" and so on and so on, always ordered by the board never by number, as Henry would know exactly how many items a wareboard would hold. He would reply with a series of grunts never writing anything down and always seeming to remember the lot!

Barry Pascoe, as mentioned previously, took on as wheelman after Henry Venn and continued until his retirement in 1959. Barry was a small man but with long arms and huge hands! All his working life was spent either at Venn's Pottery before closure then with Lakes until retirement. Barry was also the kiln packer when the old kiln was in use prior to 1946. He was ideally suited to this task as the large pitchers were fired neck down in rings around the kiln chamber, starting at the centre and it finished with Barry lying face down on the 'ledge' and lowering pitchers by spanning the bases with one large hand and placing them on to a brick – no mean feat with only candles to work with.

The layout of the making shop consisted of the wareboard store at one end. They were all nine foot long and of varying widths with the wedging bench against the mill house wall. This was made of very heavy ex-ship's timbers and necessarily very strongly made. The wheel itself consisted of frame, spindle with pulley at bottom end and at the top a large cast iron wheel 'head' surrounded by the water box. These 'heads' were changed to much larger versions when needed for larger pans, etc., the largest being about twenty inches across.

Before the Leach pottery even started in St Ives, Bernard Leach visited the pottery in Truro with his two sons and Homada who became a famous Japanese potter. Seen here in the 1920s Barry Pascoe is showing them how to put handles on pots.

This old wheel was driven by an endless rope from the bottom pulley, the motive power being a large drive wheel similar to a cartwheel with side rims mounted in a heavy timber frame and turned by a central handle by the wheel 'boy'. This lad was very skilled as he controlled the differing wheel speeds required by the wheelman. In summer time the rope would have to be kept wet to stop it slipping on the wooden drive wheel.

During the early 1930s this method of rotation was changed, and the rope drive was discontinued. Gearing was added to the spindle end, a large handle similar to a mangle was mounted on the side, this still being turned by the wheel boy. This wheel was then superseded by a large kick wheel operated by the wheelman himself. This wheel continued in use until electrical power was connected just prior to 1940 when a large motor driven Boulton double cone wheel was brought into use and was the main production wheel until the pottery closed. This wheel was driven by an endless flat belt passing through the wall to the motor in a housing outside in the yard.

The tools used by the wheelman were very simple, a selection of flat 'spoons' rectangular and varying from four inches by three inches to smaller tongue spoons with curved ends, made of iron by Mitchells the blacksmiths in Kenwyn Street, all with a hole in the centre so they could be gripped when slippery with clay. Brass wire cutters were used for releasing pots from the wheel head. Rabbit snare wire was used and short lengths of furze wood for handles. The iron wheel heads would wear down with the abrasive action of the clay, hands and the use of the spoons and occasionally have to go to an engineer to be cut back to flat on a lathe. The spoons themselves through constant use would become very sharp on the corners and edges and would be the cause of many a nasty cut [to the] hand. The sharp edges would be removed by rubbing the spoons on the wall outside. The resulting grooves were still on the wall when the building was demolished in recent years. The measurements to which all the ware was made were by means of 'sticks', i.e. the pot stick, the pitcher stick and the pan stick, etc. These sticks up to about two feet long and one and a half inches wide and half an inch thick were notched on both sides – one side for heights and the other for the widths. [It was] very simple and very accurate, a rule was never used and nothing was ever written down. The wheel gauges, pointed lengths of wood, were stuck on to the wheel box with a lump of clay and 'set' at the beginning of each run of shapes, usually just one for height and width with occasionally a second one for a wide belly. The making shop was also the point of another operation, that of 'bawing' or the application of 'pulled' handles. The Lakes pitcher range was very popular and a tremendous amount of them were made of all seven sizes, more of which later. Long before the days of plastic buckets, etc. the pitcher was the most common item in Cornish kitchens. With mostly well water in country areas, the large pitchers were used for collecting and storing water and had to be of strong manufacture. The handles especially would have to be applied at exactly the right time to bond properly. Mr Russell Matthews carried out all the 'bawing' operations, he was another man who spent his entire working life, apart from war service, at the pottery. Lakes pitcher handles were all finished by a plain 'rubbed in' tail. The thumb point finish was confined to the 'fancy' range of jugs. All the wares final finishing was carried out in the making shop, the base scraping and stamping, sponging of all the fancy ware range, all the jobs that had to be done on a tremendous range of ware. In later years all this work was carried out in the bawing shed to be built next to the firehouse at the other side of the yard.

The pottery was at that time the only manufacturer of cloam ovens in the county. These ovens were very popular with older country folk and would be found built into the hearth of many a cottage and farmhouse. Of very robust construction, they varied in size from quite small, i.e. enough room to bake a couple of loaves, to a very large oven measuring some two feet six inches across the front and nearly three feet long. The small one was labelled a 'one peck' and the largest a 'five peck'. The pecks would be gouge marks just above the door. The doors of the small ovens would have a single handle and on the larger sizes double handles were attached. The walls of all these ovens were around one and a half inches thick so were very heavy to handle when dry. The domed top and rear of a Lakes oven was very distinctive, as was the decoration applied to the dome. On larger ovens thin strips of clay would be applied in lines and 'thumbed', on smaller ones a notched roller would be used for decoration. The need for these decorations must have been traditional only because once built into the hearth wall nothing would be seen of the oven except the flat wall and door!

The ovens were built of 'sanded' clay, in effect any old contaminated or very soft clay that could not be used for anything else! The oven clay was stored against the wall near the well, and coarse sand was stored in a little cubby hole next to the mill, with a hatchway to Bosvigo Road. This sand would be mixed up with the clay to 'open' it, so that it would not distort in the firing. This was the boys' job, also to carry it up the stairs to the oven platt in the barn. Here the base would be laid and a start made on building up the walls. As the walls came higher the inside was supported by anything that came to hand, old newspapers, straw, etc. The wall would be built up using handfuls of clay at a time and beaten into shape using a wooden 'bat' not unlike a butter pat. This operation would take some days as clay previously added had to be allowed to dry a little before the next application. The flat front, or door wall, was raised at the same time, the door being cut out with a long knife and angled inwards on the sides. This ensured a final and individual tight fit when in use. Handles would now be 'pulled' or 'bawed' as with the pitchers. The dome would now be completed, still being supported by material on the inside. Decoration, etc. followed, the oven then being left for a considerable time to dry thoroughly. Several ovens of course would be built and in different stages of drying, so that there were normally one or two ready for the monthly firing. The last two ovens made at the pottery during the 1950s were made by Russell Matthews and were of one peck size. One went to the County Museum in Truro, the other to the British Museum in London. During the 1980s, whilst working at the Bolingey Pottery at Perranporth, I had the job of restoring a large five-peck oven removed from a local farmhouse and making a new

45

two-handled door. This oven is now on show at the Perranzabuloe Museum.

'Crease' or ridge tiles were also made in rectangular moulds of about 18 inches long, also of sanded clay, as were 'deckle top' decorative garden tiles used for edging borders and paths. Eight inches tall and twelve inches long, these were very popular and were last made during the late 1950s. I still see them from time to time in old established gardens.

The Drying Process was critical and as fast as possible to maintain a supply of dry ware for firing each month. When 'dressed', small ware could be dried fairly quickly, larger wares very slowly as sudden drying would cause distortion and cracked bases. This was done outside in the yard if dry enough, all the year round, but not in direct sunlight. An empty wareboard would be placed across the exposed tops of pots to keep the sun off. To save space flowerpots would be 'greaped up'.

Matt pulling a snake handle (one of three) on a pot. This was an old Lakes speciality.

Greaping involved placing one inside another, eight inch pots would be in twos only, seven inch in threes, six inch and below in fours and would remain so

through drying and firing. The pots over eight inches would be stacked for drying purposes, four or five high, base to base and rim to rim and just previous to firing would be 'nested', i.e. a twelve inch pot would contain a ten inch – eight inch – six inch – four inch. A five inch and seven inch would be inside a nine inch pot. They would be fired in these groups when dry. The 'firehouse' opposite to the making shop, was a large cob walled building with a double door and no windows, very dark and always smokey black. Strong wooden 'rails' would hold enough loaded wareboards stacked right to the roof to fill the kiln. When using the highest of the sets of rails, empty boards would be passed upwards, then all the ware to be dried would be carefully handed up to someone perched on a ladder in the smokey hot atmosphere to stack on to the empty wareboards. The heat was provided by heaps of 'glaws' on the slab floor. The kiln in those days used mostly furze from the two furze ricks in the yard and there were always many wheelbarrows full of prickles. They were gathered up and used to heat the firehouse. Like mini bonfires they burned continuously making a sort of glowing charcoal heap, topped up now and again with fresh prickles. They were a cheap source of slow heat ideal for the purpose. This method of drying ware was employed until 1946 when the coal burning kiln was built. Furze being difficult to obtain, a coke boiler was then installed with hot water pipes, to do the same job.

The kiln in use prior to 1946 was the stone built brick lined up draught bottle kiln situated at the rear of the property, the stack protruding through the roof of the building adjoining Bosvigo Road. The loading door being level with the first floor of the main building, this large area floored with ex-ship's timber from Falmouth docks was named the 'barn'. It was extensively used to dry ware prior to firing and to store fired ware prior to sale, the difficulty being of course moving all the ware for firing, up one flight of stairs! Just at the top of these stairs next to the wall was the 'oven platt', an area where all the cloam ovens were made, necessarily not too far away from the loading door of the kiln as the larger of the ovens when dry would weigh around one hundredweight and was very difficult to manoeuvre into the kiln for firing. The manufacture of these ovens has previously been mentioned. The expansion bands that held the kiln structure together were heavy chains also purloined apparently from Falmouth docks! The loading doors were of heavy iron. Inside at door level was a circular 'shelf' or gallery some eighteen inches wide above which the dome of the kiln rose up to the stack and smoke outlet. Beneath was the main firing chamber some eight feet deep and ten feet across, the floor of which was made up of firebrick slabs and semi circular firebrick sections with gaps between, which covered the flame ingress from the fire eyes outside. Those sections were believed to have been purloined from the old Truro Gas Works retort house when [it was] refurbished. The kiln packer Barry Pascoe and a couple of boys to pass in the ware would 'go kil' early on the Monday morning. Firing would start at around 7a.m. the following Friday and continue throughout the night until about 9a.m. on the Saturday. Barry would start packing by means of 'rings' next to the chamber walls starting with nested flowerpots on the outer rings then large pitchers upside down on bricks, filling as high as was within reach. The large dry pots would be spanned with a short board and would easily take the weight of the packer standing on them. Packing would continue upward in rings, heavy items – cloam ovens, etc. – would be in the centre. When the height of the shelf was reached packing would be from the centre outwards, Barry lying down or standing again on boards spanning the ware as this level rose upward. Very heavy firebrick slabs some 4–5 inches thick would be built as a wall on the edge of the shelf and would be raised upwards with the packing of the ware, gradually tilting inwards, to make, in effect, a temporary dome or hovel. On getting as high as possible in the chamber, the topmost layer of pots would be 'capped' with large 'shards' or broken pots. The packer's job now finished, the main doors would be closed and sealed with scrap clay and firing would commence.

Sometimes, depending on what ware was within, i.e. an unusual amount of very large items, a slow 'soak' was necessary on the Thursday evening, prior to proper burning on the Friday. The fire 'eyes' would be prepared, the fire bars erected on piles of fire bricks were ex locomotive fire bars 'borrowed' from G.W.R. Lit with furze faggots coal would be used for the first part of the firing – special long flame coal in large lumps was used. This went on to about midnight, coal having been previously stacked ready to use adjacent to the fire eyes and shovelled into the fire when needed by long handled shovels. Two other men would take over at midnight. The red hot fire bars would be knocked out and removed by means of long iron rakes then the furze would be thrust into the eyes, whole faggots at a time, with special 'pikes', the ends being not unlike horseshoes on long handles. The combustion was tremendous, flames normally to be seen emerging from the stack some twenty five feet above the eyes and was a familiar sight by night to the local population.

Testing was carried out by looking through the 'spies', loose bricks in the kiln wall at differing heights with an aperture through into the glowing interior where a strategically placed glazed pot had been left on its side so that by looking through the spy the men could see the run of the glaze and estimate the time to stop stoking.

By now many hundreds of furze faggots would have been used. The area round the base of the kiln would be very hot and smokey, the men sustaining themselves with water from pitchers and being very glad when the decision was made to 'close up'. The eyes would be covered with more slabs and everybody went home, usually early on the Saturday morning, to return on the Monday to unload the still very hot kiln. The ware would be stored in the large barn at the same level as the doors, or else taken downstairs to be loaded on the delivery wagon driven by Bill Collins.

One very important ingredient of this operation of course was the constant supply of furze. A man was employed full time to ensure a good supply, mostly from the Polgoda Downs area near Goonhavern but sometimes from areas all round Truro. The faggots were about five feet long and eighteen inches thick, the bushy ends alternate and bound in the centre with a willow wand twisted to form a knot. The faggots would be 'ricked up' at the cutting site until ready for collection by wagon (or lorry in later years) and brought into the pottery yard where two huge ricks were constantly part of the scene. The old men used to reckon they could tell what time of the year any pitcher was fired because of the variation in the glaze owing to the sap content of the furze used!

[This provides] a picture then of just how the original Lakes Pottery carried out its operations at Chapel Hill from 1914–1946 when many changes were made. I joined the pottery in 1948 and many years of working with both Barry Pascoe and Russell Matthews who had been at the pottery all their working lives has enabled me to write of their experiences and stories over such a long time. Mr Bill Lake and Mrs Lake, who dealt mostly with the sales side of the pottery, also helped with the details from his father and his grandfather's time. The old gentlemen were all 'characters' in their own right although the hours worked were very long and the work hard and some very injurious to their health. They kept a wonderfully philosophical sense of humour and stories abounded such as 'the market day'.

In the days when animals were driven through the streets of Truro to the market at the top of Castle Hill a herd of bullocks invaded the yard which was full of wareboards of drying pots! Everything was ruined and had to be made again. Then there was the elderly and for the most part inebriated member of staff living in nearby Kenwyn Street, who, upon being woken up in the early hours by the 'boy' to finish firing the kiln, would have to be wheeled up the street to the pottery in a wheelbarrow! Lovely stories from dear old craftsmen.

I joined the staff of the pottery in September 1948 straight from Truro Secondary Modern School, where I had enjoyed one afternoon per week of pottery lessons at *the old Truro Art School that formed part of the same building in Union Place (now the Public Library). The tutor in those days was Mr Bob Ragg who had his own studio pottery at Idless and also Mr Homer, late of the Wayside Pottery at St. Agnes. Although the working practices as described previously had not changed very much, the premises and equipment were 'brought up to date' just after the war years, most significant being that of the new kiln, built on the lower part of the yard in 1944. This brick built kiln was a familiar landmark in that area of Truro, its tall domed stack standing out above the rooftops of the surrounding buildings but sadly demolished in the late 1980s, not having been used for many years and becoming dangerous.*

The clay still from Fishley Hollands pit at Fremington, North Devon, was going through a 'dirty' patch at that time and Mr Bill Lake the boss decided to invest in a filter press, to 'clean' the clay before use. The limestone content, always a problem, had got much worse and a lot of finished ware had to be discarded owing to the tiny limestones in the clay body expanding during firing and thus pitting the surface. The filter press built by Boultons of Stoke on Trent was installed in 1948–9. In the mill house the old pug mill was still churning out 'spits' now driven by an overhead electric motor through a large oil filled open top gearing system. The poor old horses were disposed of many years before. The operations in the clay pit were the same, soaked clay being carried in by shovel to form 'batches but then fed into a large rotary 'blunger' with water from a new underground tank to render it to 'slip' or liquid clay. It was then put through a vibrating screen to remove the stones and dropped into a large tank which was agitated constantly to avoid settlement. The liquid clay would then be pumped into the filter press, itself a system of large rectangular plates with canvas (later nylon) covers. The plates being concave, with holes in the bottom, were fed under pressure by a central hole, the clean clay forming on the canvas with excess water leaving via the holes at the bottom of the plates, which were some four feet square and held at their sides on cast iron rails, some twenty four plates all held together with heavy eight foot long bolts at the corners.

This pressing operation would take all day, the plates being emptied first thing in the morning, and the formed plates of clay dropping on to a special truck under the press, as the cast iron plates were moved to release them. The empty plates would then be bolted together again to be refilled under pressure of around one hundred and eighty pounds per square inch. The glaze used for all pitchers and domestic ware was then blue lead galena, made up from dry powdered lead and slip (liquid clay), the proportions of which I forget although I remember several gullies full of slip were

called for. Barry Pascoe, then the 'metaller', would make the glaze up in an old cast iron wash boiler built against the firehouse wall and a little clay saucer like float was used to determine the density. On one occasion when the newly installed filter press was brought into use, Barry, who must have been busy at the time, entrusted the task of making the slip for the glaze to a new boy. Making the slip was quite hard work so it was suggested that some be drawn off the filter press. Immediately behind the press on the pipework was a large tap, under which the lad held his pitcher and on turning the tap on full, the pressure being around one hundred and eighty pounds, [he was left] with only one handle in his hand, the rest in pieces on the floor with slip flying everywhere. The resulting comments from Barry upon being presented with merely a handle by a crestfallen youth are not recorded! The whole machine was powered by a ten horsepower electric motor and driven by a continuous flat belt from the floor above. The 'clean' clay plates were then stacked and covered with damp sacking until fed into the pug mill for further preparation by the wedger. In later years a smaller wall mounted pug mill was installed near the wedger's bench in the making shop, to further assist in clay preparation for the wheels. A second electric double cone wheel was installed also in 1949.

A word now about the staff at the pottery at that time. Mr and Mrs Bill Lake were the proprietors, Mrs Lake's sister Miss Joan Collins ran the recently started colour glazing department, Miss Powning was the secretary, Barry Pascoe was wheelman and metaller, Russell Matthews was clay pit, handles, ware dressing and kiln man, Fred Coward was wedger, George Wright was in charge of the mill and press, Harold (Sam) Hankins was yard man and general assistant and I was the boy! With Miss Collins were Kath Carson, Vera Pollard and my late wife Stella. Stella was shortly to take over the colour section on the retirement of Joan Collins. There was a succession of colour girls whose names I cannot recall. I was now put to work to learn my trade as second wheelman. To watch Barry working, a fine craftsman, was all the tuition I would ever receive! Taciturn to say the least, Barry would only answer questions with a grunt but after many months I was able to make to his satisfaction and continued to make all the fancy ware, etc. until leaving the pottery in 1958. On Barry Pascoe's retirement, Matt (Russell Matthews) took over as senior wheelman, making all the larger items. Matt worked at the pottery all his life apart from Army service; a fine craftsman and a dear friend. He was still head potter when the firm changed hands. He retired in the early '70s and died soon afterwards.

The premises in my time included an office and showroom immediately to the right on entering the yard

Russell (Matt) Matthews, Stella Edwards and Harold (Sam) Hankins, all three now sadly deceased, outside at Lakes Pottery in 1950.

and adjoining the old stable which had an original cobbled floor and was used for fancy ware storage. The cart and wagon house next door was brought into use as a bulk store for the new kiln. The kiln building itself, a large covered area, encircling the kiln and stretching back to the boundary wall, was for ware storage prior to firing. Wide shelving to store the very large items was attached to the rear wall made from the now redundant wareboards. This area set closer to the kiln was used to stack the 'saggers', the earthenware boxes which when full of small items for biscuit firing formed the bottom half of the kiln chamber, more of which later. Immediately to the left on entering the gate were the three 'bays' with 'pin' posts, pins made of lengths of pipe fitting into a series of holes in heavy vertical timbers thus providing a drying area for ware, the boards being held on two 'pins' at whatever height was needed. Later the new office was built in the end bay nearer the gate, thus making a larger showroom across the yard. At the end of these bays was the old garage, now housing a Catterson Smith Trolley Hearth Electric Kiln. This kiln was installed to fire the smaller colour items from the new fancyware section at the top of the stairs rising behind the kiln. This glazing and decorating section was quite extensive, consisting of workroom, glaze store and biscuit ware store. This long department was above the three bays mentioned previously.

The electric kiln was in use continually, with normally three firings per week, overnight, turning out a wide selection of colour glaze items and slipware.

The next workshop was the 'Bawing' shed, also equipped with 'pin posts', with a zinc covered bench which Russell Matthews would cover from end to end with clay 'pulls' to start a day's handling, a jug at a time. On a brick on the bench he would handle a full wareboard of some forty jugs in a very short space of time, whilst I, still learning the art, would maybe complete six!

Mike Edwards is hard at work on his power wheel which was situated in front of Barry Pascoe's wheel. The power wheel was bought new from Boultons in 1950.

'Dressing', i.e. bottom scraping, stamping and final sponging, also took place in this shed next to the fire house. The area in the corner behind the firehouse, where once stood a furze rick was now the store for flowerpots awaiting delivery or collection. The 'barn' up the stairs and over the mill was a store for finished items and packing materials, tea chests, etc. and also a store for biscuit ware awaiting colour glazing by the girls in their department.

The new kiln was built, as previously stated, in 1944. The structure itself and the six sided surrounding building was built of red brick. Kiln builders and bricklayers were brought in from Stoke on Trent to undertake this somewhat specialist task. The stack, some thirty feet high, tapered inward from where the kiln emerged from the flat concrete roof of the surrounding building being some fifteen feet in diameter at this point, to the final top cap of three feet. The inner lining and the domed top-firing chamber, with its sides and central dampers, was made of firebrick. The portion of the structure below roof level was 'stepped out' for strength, the walls being some three feet thick at the base, which was some twenty feet in diameter. These 'steps' supported the six inch wide steel expansion bands made of three sections with flanges which bolted together. Five of these bands were in position, one at the very top of the stack, two above the roof level where the end of the vertical walls finished and the tapered section began and two below roof level inside the building. Such was the expansion pressure when the kiln was hot that at an early firing one one inch thick bolt, being one of three securing a joint, sheared off and was found in the street some distance away! Perhaps it was just as well it happened late at night when nobody was about. These steel bands were periodically checked by insurance inspectors and had to be kept painted with red oxide every year. Getting up to the very top to paint was no easy job! The band which spanned the loading door was joined by a heavy removable section, put in place for each firing after the door had been bricked up with double thickness of firebricks, using liquid clay as mortar. This section would then have to be tightened with a huge spanner. Five fire 'eyes' of arched construction were spaced around the base of the kiln. Under fire bar level was below ground with access via a pit with boards to walk on. The eyes themselves were some five feet in length and three feet wide, the stoking hole being three feet above floor level and only large enough for a shovel of coal. This aperture was closed off with a large earthenware slab which was slid to one side with a shovel during stoking, as the slab would become red hot! The flame from the coal being burnt would travel into the interior of the kiln through small 'galleries' at the rear of the eye, some going under the floor to emerge through channels in the brickwork, others channelled upwards to emerge through the lower part of the side walls. The coal would have been brought in from the nearby coal store by wheelbarrows and enough for the firing, about four to five tons, would be heaped against the outer building walls near to each fire eye.

The kiln was packed by Russell Matthews with Sam Hankins and myself tending. First went the saggers, about one hundred earthenware boxes of different shapes and sizes filled with all manner of non glazed items. These would be built to six feet high then topped off with large 'covers' of firebrick then the pack would commence as in the old kiln, 'rings' of nested pots, pitchers on their necks, etc. to just short of the dome. To allow for expansion, the height of the packing above 'cover' level was about nine to ten feet

at the centre, the section next to the door completed last. The door was bricked up, the band joined up, top dampers all open (these being reached by a long iron hook through an access hatch outside on the roof at the base of the dome), 'spy irons' in place (long iron rods with glazed clay on the tips inserted through holes in the brickwork into spaces left when packing) and we were ready for firing.

Light up with some furze, wood and coal, 7.30 Friday morning. Bill Lake would shout over the wall to the little terrace of cottages bordering Bosvigo Road, "Mind your washing, my dears, we're burning today!" A great scurrying of housewives would follow, gathering in the sheets and washing from all the clothes lines before the smuts fell and ruined the fruits of their labours. Smoke was so thick in the kiln building, we had to be careful not to fall in the by then uncovered pits! "All going" was the shout, to emerge from the gloom coughing and spluttering. After a while when the up draught started to pull, the smoke would clear. Matt would take the firing through the day, stoking each eye with two or three shovelfuls every quarter hour. At 5.30p.m. Mr Lake and Sam would do first turn to midnight, the atmosphere getting hot by now! Matt and myself would take over for the late turn, Matt shovelling three eyes, myself the other two, by now very hot and hard work. Matt inspecting the 'spies' regularly through the night, at about 7a.m. would announce "'Tis done, I'll ring the boss". Summoned from his house up the road, Mr Lake would shortly arrive and agree that "'Tis time to close up", so up on the roof we would go, open up the top hatch and using the long iron hook across the red hot area above the dome, slide the top dampers across to keep the heat in. No more shovelling – and home we went, filthy dirty and with the roaring of the fires at full draught ringing in our ears.

Monday morning we would open the dampers again to cool the interior, take down the bricks in the doorway, then start unpacking, taking all day with four men. All the ware was stacked up in the kiln building, soon to be moved to the various store areas around the premises. The following day or so would be spent 'picking out' ware for orders, some to be packed with straw in tea chests for delivery by carrier or be taken up to the railway station on a handcart. Most, particularly plant pots, were collected by various nurserymen customers. A lot of large plant pots were always required and at the onset of the growing season, three inch pots for small tomato plants. Wednesday was always a busy day, being market day in Truro, farmers' wives were buying pitchers, pans, etc. for their kitchens. The farmers themselves calling after market for 'six penorth' of clay, this they would use to stick a little 'cup' around a loose gate hinge in an upright granite post. Some lead would be melted over a furze fire, poured into the cup to fill the hole in the granite to hold the hinge pin secure.

I feel a mention should be made of the country round vans, who used to come into the yard once a week to stock up for their visits to all the rural areas. I suppose we would call them mobile shops nowadays, then an essential part of rural life in Cornwall. Many used to call at the pottery at different times. Three I can recall all used large and usually ancient vans fitted with a large paraffin tank; they sold anything and everything except food! From the pottery they would carry a selection of pitchers and jugs, plant pots, anything the proprietors thought they could sell on their round. One van was run by Webbers of Truro, then a busy ironmongers in the city, another from Helston owned by Bawdens (?) and another from the St. Ives area driven by a real old character, who upon stopping in the yard, would leap from his van and 'borrow' an old jug or whatever, to catch the drips from his big brass tap from the paraffin tank at the back of his van. Upon leaving, these few drips would be poured back into the top of the tank and the jug would disappear into the back of the van to be followed on the next visit by another one. These he must have sold on as a small bonus!

One very good customer over the years was Mr Bert Middleton of Looe, a well known figure in that area, being in business in the town and also concerned with the then Looe Fishermans Choir. Mr Middleton would have large amounts of ware made with his own stamp on the bases, all glazed inside only, to be transported to Looe by the large load during the winter months. I believe he employed quite a few people painting the ware, using a specially formulated paint and adding 'Looe'. I remember all were blue.

I should make mention of some of the range of items produced at the pottery at that time and the somewhat peculiar names given to the pitcher range, the origins of which were never explained! The largest of the pitchers was a 'thirdall' and the next down a 'gulley'. Both these large pitchers sported a double thickness collar rim not for decoration but for strength, as previously mentioned these were fired upside down on a brick. To this day many of the old pitchers still survive with a decidedly bent rim, these were sold as seconds having been a bit over fired. The remaining pitchers were called in order of sizes the pinchgut, tivvy, the eighty, three halfpenny and the smallest the 'penny'.

Many other varieties of jug were also produced - two sizes of beer jugs, with a glazed 'bib' on the belly, two sizes of 'Truro jug, tall and straight, Malpas jugs straight with a turned out rim, Bob jugs with a very fat belly and many other smaller cream and milk jugs.

Vases were also made in a great variety, many in several sizes. Tunis vases with wide flared tops, three

handles in snake format (a very old design) vases with flat backs for wall hanging, ornamental grave capstan vases, large and small rustic crosses with notches and combed finishes, these were made in three parts and joined to form the cross. They also made mugs and beakers, poachers, egg cups, ashtrays and soap dishes, then the larger items, bread pans in two sizes, large bussas, rhubarb and kale pots, strawberry pots and large cream pans, wagon tops for chimneys, occasionally H tops (very difficult to make) and made to order chimney pots, some very large made in sections and joined. A full set, made by Barry Pascoe during the late '50s, very large two piece pots, were produced specially for use on the buildings at Walsingham Place, Truro, when the properties were restored. They are still there. Many older properties still have Lakes wagon tops on their chimneys to prevent downdraught. Another type of chimney pot was produced with side vents, made from small rounded bottom pots cut and joined on again to improve the draught. Many of these can also still be seen above the rooftops of Cornwall.

An old cottage in 1904 (possibly in the Helston area as the postcard was sent from Redruth to St Keverne) has a pitcher and a bussa in the garden.

During the late 1950s, owing to increased demand for smaller fancy coloured ware, not so many plant pots could be made so machine made pressed pots were bought in from the Royal Potteries, Weston-super-Mare. These (in our view inferior) pots were brought down by lorry, then to be unloaded through the hatchway from Bosvigo Road and stored ready for sale in the furze rick area near the old kiln.

I draw near to the end of this little account of the working practices of Lakes Cornish Pottery. My late wife and I both left the company in 1958 to move to Perranporth, my wife to look after our young family, myself to work for a period with my uncle at Godber's Nurseries and then as wheelman at Bolingey Pottery, where I stayed until its closure in 1990. I left the Truro

Pottery with many happy memories and a superb grounding in a somewhat unusual trade, which stood me in good stead throughout nearly a lifetime in the pottery production industry. Lakes was for many years the only truly commercial pottery in the county. Many 'art studio' type of potteries abounded but none could really compare with this long established company supplying the need of the local community as it did for many years.

Bernard Leach with his very young sons visited the pottery in the late 1920s before setting up his now well known pottery at St. Ives. He was apparently very interested in the techniques used by the old craftsman.

Soon after Mr Bill Lake's death in 1966 the business was sold to the Dartington Trust Venture, with a manager in charge and Mr Peter Lake heavily involved. This arrangement continued until the early 1980s when the pottery changed hands again with a Mr Hill as the new proprietor. A museum was incorporated in the premises and this continued until 1985 when falling demand finally brought permanent closure to the pottery. The premises are now used by the Truro Baptist Church.

A sad day for Truro when the pottery went up for sale. This catalogue of May Whetter and Grose lists all sorts of items from plastic buckets and lids to a gas-glazing kiln and photographs and artefacts from the museum.

Chapter 6

The Workplace

The Fire Brigade

In the early 1800s Truro had the military billeted in the town and in the event that a fire occurred they were on hand to help. However, when the soldiers had left their poorly-appointed barracks, the town found itself in need of fire fighters of some kind. The wealthier townsfolk and owners of hotels, etc. took out insurance with one of a number of companies who promised to attend a fire if and when it occurred. The Royal Hotel of today (once Pearces Hotel) for many years had the fire badge clearly visible on the wall.

By 1845 there had been a report in the paper to the effect that the fire brigade was 'not particularly active' and a stable in River Street burned down. This was the famous occasion when it was reported that the engine travelled 'at a snail's gallop' through Boscawen Street and St Nicholas Street, but only once it had taken a full 20 minutes to get it out of its garage in the coinage hall.

It was in 1868 that the Truro City Volunteer Fire Brigade was formed. Some 30 men under the command of Captain James Henderson had two fire engines and an escape that were kept in St Mary's Street. A ballot was held to recruit members and the officers were elected. At this time the men had to provide their own boots, axe and belt and W.J. Burley suggests in his centenary book of Truro that there must have been a measure of prestige in being a fireman or not many men would have been keen to do it. In order to provide the men with helmets, uniforms and the equipment they needed, funds were raised by sales and bazaars and in 1868 £575 was raised in this way – a huge amount in those days.

In 1904 the fire station was moved to Back Quay and at least one old photograph of those days shows a horse and cart standing patiently outside the entrance blocking it completely; hopefully no emergency arose! In 1927 the first motorised appliance arrived and in keeping with the tradition started then, the name for the appliance, 'The City of Truro', is still in use today. During the same year there was an explosion in the

Members of the fire brigade c.1930 on Lemon Quay.

gas holder in Fairmantle Street. Ray Hobbs remembers it well although he was only a schoolboy and he noted that people came running out with their hair on fire and singed eyebrows. The marvellous motorised appliance attended but there was only one casualty and he was not seriously hurt. Mr Burley tells us:

... a delivery man was trapped by his van which had been turned over by the blast. A well-known Truro figure of the time went up to the trapped man, tapped him on the shoulder and said, 'I should get up if I was you, mate, they say t'other one's going up any minute.'

The National Fire Service came into being with the Second World War and by 1944 had a new fire station in St George's Road, but today the headquarters is in the Old County Hall.

Rickard's Temperance Hotel

TRURO.

W. ROBINS, Proprietor.

LUNCHEONS   TEA ROOMS

Bed and Breakfast - - - - 3 -
Hot and Cold Luncheons daily, 6d. to 1/-

EXCURSIONISTS CATERED FOR.

Left: *Not only was Clyma's Hotel a temperance hotel situated in River Street but Rickard's was also a temperance hotel lower down River Street towards Victoria Place.*

Right: *Clyma's Hotel used to be in River Street opposite the Baptist chapel and for many years in more recent memory before its closure it was the Imperial Hotel. Clyma's was a temperance hotel and was advertised as being not only an easy distance from the railway station, cathedral and Post Office but also five minutes' walk from the landing-stage.*

CLYMA'S HOTEL

(UNLICENSED)

RIVER STREET, TRURO.

Situated in the main thoroughfare from the Station and five minutes' walk from the Cathedral, Post Office and Landing Stage.

THE MOST CENTRAL HOTEL FOR TOURISTS, MOTORISTS, CYCLISTS, etc.

Recommended by the Motor Union.

Garage adjoining.   Dark Room.   Terms moderate.

J. H. SAUNDERS,

Shipping Agent and Agent for the Polytechnic Touring Association.

Passages booked to United States, Canada, South Africa, Australia and most parts of the World.

Left: *Part of the training for every fire fighter involved a rescue by helicopter and John Allam is seen here being winched to safety.*

Below: *It is possible Truro had a lucky escape as this is the proposed installation of continuous vertical retorts for the gas board to erect on the site of the old gasworks. It was a modern system for discharging coal and loading coke onto ships which would be anchored at a new wharf. If this system had been adopted it might have been difficult to tell which was a more imposing edifice on the skyline of Truro, the cathedral or the gasworks!*

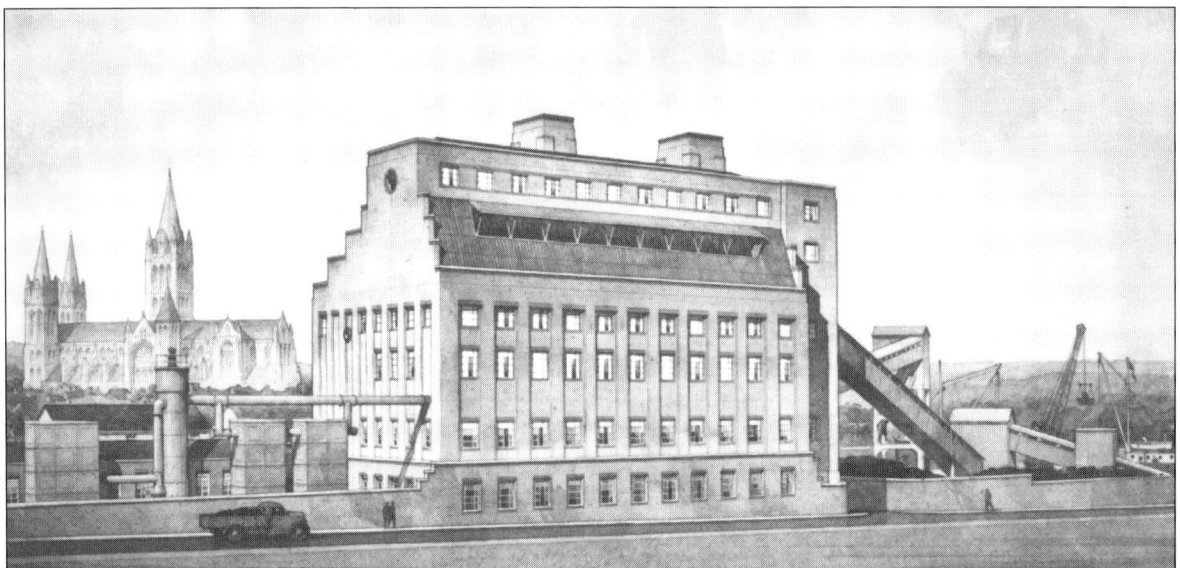

When not attending fires or other incidents which required the services of the fire brigade, there was time to catch up with the news. Cyril Anstis relaxes at the fire station at St George's Road, c.1955.

Walter Penfold takes a turn in the chair outside the waiting room.

The Police Force

Truro Borough Police Force was run on the Metropolitan style of policing and in 1839 five constables were sworn in, along with an inspector who came from London. As far back as 1822 the Mayor had tried to raise a force to deal with the 'frequent occurrence of night broils in the street' but, as is the way of local government, it took a while to organise. Sir Robert Peel founded the Metropolitan Police Force in 1829 but it was the Municipal Corporations Act of 1835 which stated that the new corporations should raise a watch committee that led to the formation of the force.

The police station was in the Municipal Buildings as was the magistrates court which was in the Town Hall, and so the threat to miscreants of 'I'll have you under the clock' meant just that, as the town clock sits solidly on top of the Municipal Buildings. (There was, however, an occasion when it did not as there was a serious fire in 1914 which completely destroyed the clock tower which fell down into the council chamber beneath. An anonymous donor paid for a replacement and

an identical tower was built, the only difference being that the clock face on the replacement was white and not black.)

The Cornwall Constabulary was formed in 1857 and at some time after that a police station was built in the Trafalgar area of the town. Because the borough force existed and dealt with the city, the county constabulary had no jurisdiction within the city limits. Police pay was not good and it is recorded that in 1878 Superintendent Angel received an annual amount of £108. Woolcock, a 'town sergeant', received £61.4s.0d. per annum. Although these sums did not constitute good pay it was the same story in every police force throughout the country. Superintendent Angel's remuneration was only slightly more than the amount which Superintendent Nash had received 20 years earlier. By 1914, the same year that the clock tower burnt down, a constable joining the force was paid 18s.0d. per week, whereas in 1856, just before the formation of the Cornwall Constabulary, a constable would have been paid 14s.6d., just 3s.6d. less – there was not much inflation in those days! In 1919 His Majesty's Inspector of Constabularies recommended a merger

Workmen dig up Boscawen Street in February 1966. It seemed at one time that the road was always being disturbed; as soon as one utility had replaced cables or pipes, along would come another company needing to dig it up again to repair their equipment. These days it seems to be better organised but whenever the road does come up the size of the granite setts often causes surprise.

with the county force which took place rather later in March 1921.

When Sam Oatey was stationed in Truro just before, during and after the war years, he had plenty to do being the officer who had to organise the demolition of unexploded bombs and also being the driver of one of the very few patrol cars (the first one in Truro.) There were many things he remembered over the course of a whole career but there were two things he particularly spoke of dating from his time in Truro. He was a very musical person and was proud to say that he had met the famous pianist, Myra Hess, who had come to Truro to give a concert. Unfortunately it was in less than ideal circumstances as far as the lady was concerned as she came across Sam after her fur coat was stolen and he was put on the case. As it was so long ago no one can remember now whether the coat ever turned up or not. The other thing which particularly stuck in Sam's mind was the fact that when the Prince of Wales (later the uncrowned Edward VIII) came to visit some of the

Duchy farms and Sam had to escort him. At one farm there was a peppercorn rent to pay and in this case a scoop of peppercorns was offered to the Prince who had no idea what they were or what he should do with them – so he asked Sam's advice!

Jack Parnell was a master barber with a barber's shop in Lower Lemon Street in the late 1930s. He later moved to premises in Cathedral Lane and among his customers was the late Lord Falmouth. It was a matter of pride that every customer that came into the shop had a clean towel to drape around himself and Jack's wife Betty recalled in later years how difficult it used to be for her. At that time she had four small children and they generated plenty of washing for someone without the washing machine and dryer that most people take for granted today. Added to her normal wash would be a pure white huckaback towel for every customer that had been into the shop that day so that meant another wash to be done after the children were in bed. It was tough going to get all the towels dry, especially in winter.

Another business (which had an aroma to remind one of its existence) was the Furniss factory. John Cooper Furniss started his bakery business in King Street and later moved to Cathedral Lane, at that time called Church Lane, where as well as his usual customers, he catered for the hungry workers who were engaged in the building of the cathedral. He also ran the railway station buffet and often his cart was pushed up Richmond Hill full of good food destined for the passengers on the new railway system. By 1887 he had retired from the board and he died in 1888, but the factory lived on and delighted the residents of Truro with the smell of gingerbread, peppermint rock and humbugs for many years to come. When the factory was finally moved to Redruth the citizens felt they had lost something special. Some 100 shares in his company were left to the city council to provide coal in winter for the needy but so many people these days have alternative forms of heating that the councillors have difficulty in giving the coal vouchers away.

When Frederick Woodward Mitchell came back from the First World War having been gassed at Ypres he decided that he would set up in his trade as a blacksmith and farrier in Kenwyn Street. On 31 December 1921 his name was entered on the roll of the Worshipful Company of Farriers and for many years his certificate was folded in a drawer in the smithy getting covered in soot and grime. The premises he rented at 108 Kenwyn Street had a yard laid in cobbles which had been put there by the friars in the thirteenth century and he carried on his business there for many years. Later he was joined by his son

This is a photograph of the Truro City Police Force which was presented to Mr Alderman W.A. Phillips who was the Mayor of Truro 1919–20. It was presented by the Chief Constable, Sergeants and Constables 'as a token of their esteem and as a memento of the Force as constituted during his Mayoralty.'

Left: Police constable Sam Oatey was PC 57 in the Cornwall Constabulary. Although this photo was taken early on in his career, by the time he was posted to Truro during the war years he had had a variety of experiences. He had been the deputy Chief Constable's driver (this was when the Cornwall Constabulary had its head-quarters in Bodmin), and when in Truro he drove one of the first patrol cars and was the Bomb Reconnaissance Officer.

Below: In May 1972 work was under way on the new Roman Catholic Church of Our Lady of the Portal and St Piran in St Austell Street. The old church was in Chapel Hill.

Left: *One of the things that most Truronians have done in their time is to have climbed to the top of Victoria tower, the highest of the cathedral towers. It was c.1930 that schoolboy Cyril Lanxon was taken up the tower and came face to face with the steeplejack. Cyril had his Brownie box camera with him and took this amazing photograph. For many years the same family of steeplejacks have been employed at the cathedral. They are called Dawson. This intrepid gentleman is sitting on a type of home-made swing way above the old south aisle with a collar and tie under his dungarees and not even a hard helmet to protect his head.*

Right: *Remarkably few photos of the Furniss biscuit factory survive – not even the company have any – but Andy McNally, their representative, kindly allowed the author to photocopy his copy of their brochure from the 1970s. This picture shows the biscuits on the production line being inspected by Roy Lean and Bill Thomas while Valerie Osborne is more camera conscious!*

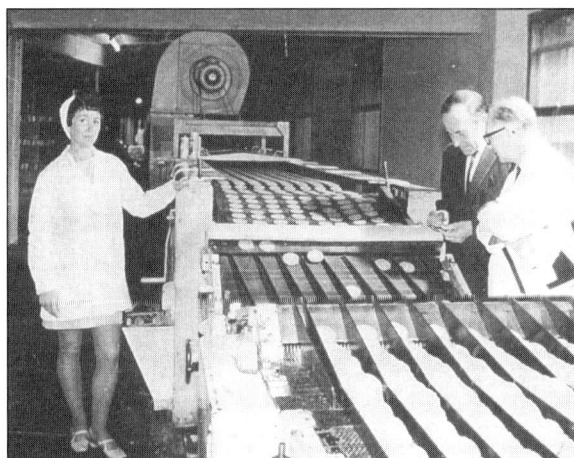

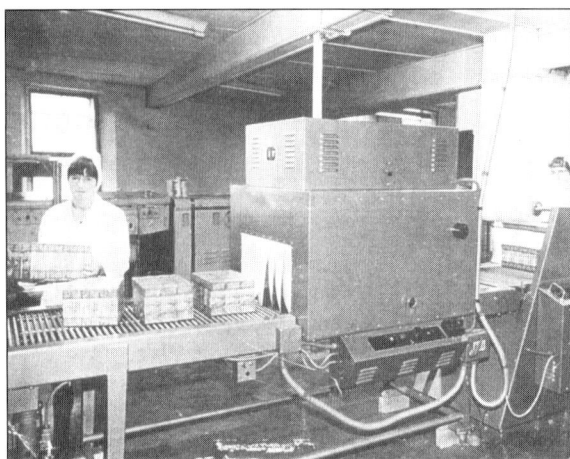

Sylvia Pascoe was on the production line to collect the goods after all the biscuits had been wrapped and boxed.

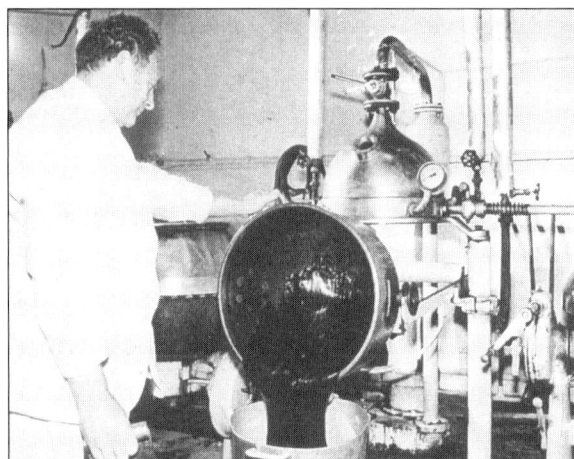

Not only did Furniss make biscuits but also boiled sweets and peppermint rock. In the photograph we see Bill Collins carefully pouring the sticky mixture into a pan. At one time the company produced sweets known as Tom Trots and often they were sold in a tin with a picture of 'Tom Trot' on it. It is believed that the factory foreman Douglas Edward Murton was the model for Tom.

Fred and then by Byryn, another son who had left school a few days before and expected to be having a rare treat and going to stay for a brief summer holiday with an aunt in Wembury over the Tamar in Devon. As his father needed an apprentice the holiday was cancelled! Fred senr was a member of a skittles team, had a fine voice and enjoyed a pint at the end of a busy day.

All his life there was one thing that disappointed him and his sons and that was that one Good Friday he was startled by a knocking at his door at his home in Kenwyn Street just up the road from the black-smith's shop. It was Dr Hood ready to go hunting but his horse had cast a shoe. He wanted the horse shod right away, so despite it being a bank holiday, Fred and the boys went down the road to the forge and got the fire up to the right heat to shoe the horse. It was hot and dirty work on a rare day off and no matter how many times the bill was presented, Dr Hood never paid. That sort of thing could have made a man with a wife and seven sons reluctant to help people out but he was a generous character and carried on as usual. Roughly 45 years after his death (he died in 1954) his family were told by a chance acquaintance that he had very fond memories of Fred. As a child the man had often gone to the black-smith's shop with his friends and watched enviously as they handed over their penny and saw their own hoop and stick being made. He always wanted one but knew that it was out of the question as he could not afford it – but one day Fred made an extra one and gave it to him as he did not like to see the boy left out. This was around 1930. We also know that he always helped with the harvest festival at the Standard Inn and he ordered and paid for the sheaf of harvest bread. It was made by Reg Stone after he had permission from Godfrey Tonkin of Treleaven's bakery. The stems of the sheaf were in 30–40 pieces and to make the ears of corn took as many as 400–500 pieces of bread dough. After it had been displayed with the other harvest fare it was rather dry to eat but it made a beautiful centrepiece to the display.

One day Fred received the following letter (posted on 18 December 1946) which he kept among his papers:

> Mr J Reeves
> C C C Infirmary
> No 1 Barngoose House
> Redruth Inst.
> Cornwall
>
> *Dear Old Fred*
>
> *Just a few lines to let you know Ive been waiting and waiting and just received a letter from you. I answered your letter about the Books and tobacco only the letter did not go I write it and stamp it and put it in the Cubboard in the morning when I went to the Cubboard to get the letter it was gone so I thought somebody had took the letter and posted it for me, but they must have destroyed the letter a very mean trick to do but don't matter Fred, send some more tobacco, that's how Ive been kept waiting and you have been kept waiting owing to that letter not posted. Well Fred the weather is nice and fine, but very cold over here. Well I hope you will all have a very good Christmas and all the boys and the Vic, that's all for now Fred hoping to here soon from you*
>
> *From your old Pall Joe.*

Obviously Fred kept his less fortunate friend in baccy!

A pony and jingle belonging to W. Clarke is snapped in the blacksmith's shop at 108 Kenwyn Street in 1925. Fred Mitchell has probably just shod the pony who has very trim looking hooves. The cobbles in the yard of the smithy were laid down by the Dominican friars whose land this was in the mid-thirteenth century. For many years one of the sheds behind Fred was used as a garage for a Buick motor car – quite a contrast to the horses and carts that frequented the yard.

The blacksmiths needed good relations with their neighbours as the smoke and dirt from the forge could be very messy. The cottage right next door to the entrance of their yard was where a cheerful Welsh lady lived – Mrs Penrose known as Cissy Bach. Whenever the fire was going to belch out a lot of smoke or a horse came in for shoeing, they would call over Cissy's back gate and if she had her washing out, she would nip out and pick it in. It used to seem incongruous to see a line of immaculate washing blowing out across the blacksmith's yard. Friday was Cissy's day for making Welshcakes and the boys were always delighted when she came out with a plate of them all freshly baked and covered in a clean cloth to keep them warm. Their other neighbour was Miss Osborne who ran a small grocery shop. Sometimes she would have a nice poster or map sent to her with some of her stock by way of an advertisement and she used to save them for the smiths to give to their children.

Above: *For many years the gas showrooms in Boscawen Street provided the venue for cookery demonstrations and hints and tips on how to cook with gas. This photo is c.1920 and the lady with the chef's hat is carefully stirring something on the hob.*

Below: *The servant girl handing a plate to the lady of the house is Annie Kemp who was about 38 years old at the time. Annie worked for the grandparents of Kenneth Kendall who is well known to most people through his life in broadcasting and his many television appearances. His grandparents lived in Tregolls Road which is where this photograph was taken by H. Opie and Sons.*

Taken c.1970, this photograph shows Clifford Mitchell (second from left) *and his team of cooks in the kitchens of the City Hospital. In 1981 his six-year-old great-niece Tamsin Parnell broke her arm and spent a night as an in-patient. Clifford popped in to visit during the morning and later when he looked at her modest request for lunch (she enjoyed being allowed to tick the boxes on her menu card) he decided that she had not asked for enough so he sent her a huge tray laden with one of everything! Perhaps he thought Mum and Dad sitting patiently with her looked a bit peckish!*

Chapter 7

❖

The Hospital & Health

An aerial view of the old city hospital shows just how much the building had been extended from the original structure of 1799.

It was in 1799 that Truro's new hospital was opened. Then, as now, nothing as important as that could take place without much deliberation. There were discussions as to where would be the best place to treat patients, and in Cornwall, as well as the normal accidents and illnesses that occurred, so many miners were injured in the course of their work that it was felt that a hospital was a necessity. Three of Cornwall's most influential men, Sir Francis Bassett, Sir William Lemon and Sir John Arundell, put their minds to it and the hospital came into being, perhaps rather surprisingly in Truro, not in the more concentrated mining area of Camborne and Redruth.

The list of subscribers was headed by the Prince of Wales, who contributed £500, and many other people from all walks of life donated according to their means. Dr Taunton (a noted Truro historian) was one of several who gave £5.5s. (five guineas).

Although it was a handsome building, it had its disadvantages, one of which was that it was not connected to the drains (they flowed past just outside!) and in 1878 an outbreak of typhoid claimed the life of the surgeon's wife. In 1907 a Mr Pethick of St Austell donated X-ray equipment, but in order to be able to use it he also had to have the electricity to

run it installed! This was before electricity had reached the rest of the city so it was a very modern hospital in the eyes of the populace.

During the First World War 50 beds were set aside for surgical cases of war wounded who would have mostly been from the Duke of Cornwall's Light Infantry and the governors set a charge of 2s.0d. per bed per day. By 1918 this charge had gone up to 4s.9d. per bed per day. The cost of being wounded had risen!

Tragedy struck the hospital on 6 July 1942 when two Heinkell III fighter bombers dropped two bombs on the building. They had not been detected on radar screens and no air-raid warning was given. One bomb landed on the south wing and a sister and a nurse were killed, as were three people who were visiting their relatives at the time. Carol Polglase in Maryland in the United States recalls that her cousin Flight Officer Mary Polglase died in the raid and also a Mrs Stephens, the grandmother of another Cornish exile. Peter Parnell, who was three years old at the time, remembers playing in his front garden in Courtney Road and calling to his mother that planes were dropping things in the sky. His mother Betty immediately rushed out and carried him into the shelter which occupied most of their dining-room. At the same time in Kenwyn Street, Ethel Mitchell had sent her youngest son Dennis out into the back yard to take his shoes and socks off as he had just returned from a Sunday school trip to the beach and she didn't want sand walked all over the house. Suddenly Dennis found himself lying on the yard with his father on top of him as a plane went over with bullets flying. If you know where to look the indentations can still be seen in the yard wall, although many years of whitewashing have helped to cover them. Sybil Rapsey was working in the Singer sewing-machine shop and vividly remembers the glass of the window bowing with the shock, although it did not break. Her mother, Mrs Dickinson, who lived in Station Road four doors down from the old County Hall (then the only

61

Christmas 1957 and the nurses don their capes and take to the wards to sing Christmas carols for the patients.

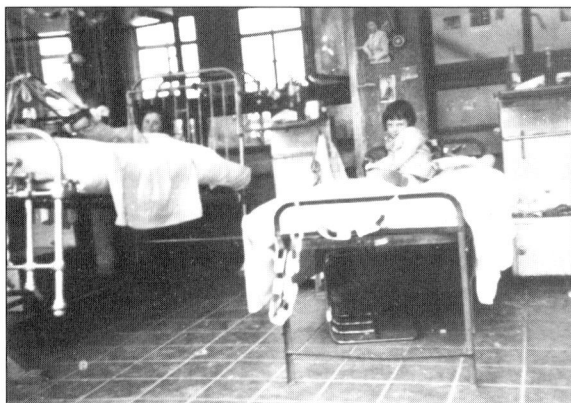

The children's ward had a balcony which had a tarpaulin that could be raised in good weather and lowered in bad conditions. This was so that the children could get plenty of fresh air. This picture was taken at the time of the coronation.

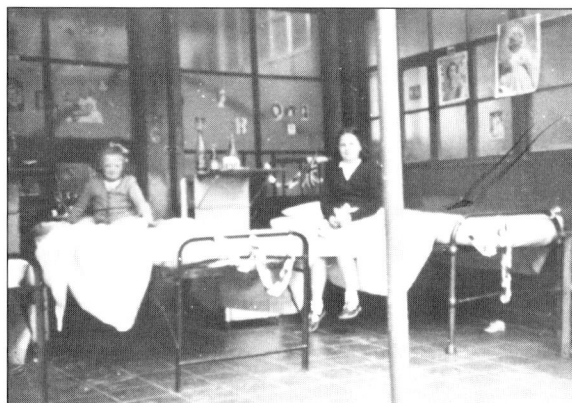

Another shot of the balcony ward as it was in 1953. It was part of the old orthopaedic ward, later the accident unit.

The first improvement to the balcony.

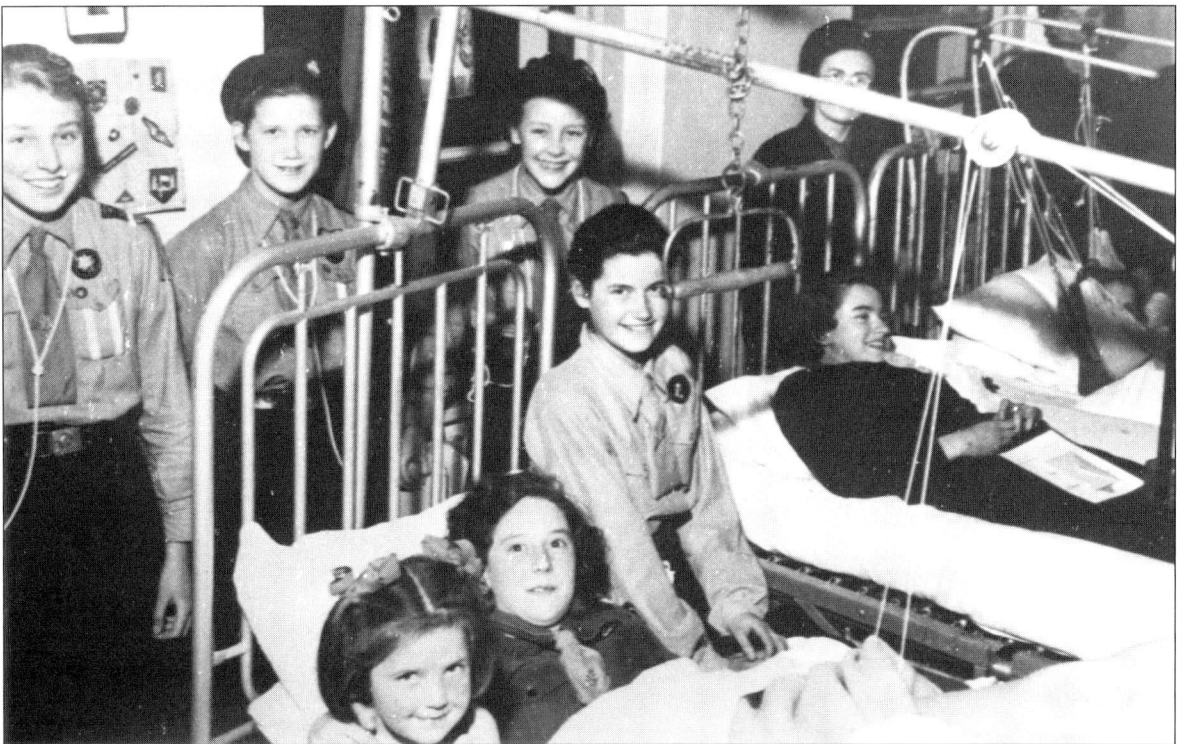

Guides and Brownies come into the ward to take part in a presentation of fortitude to Maureen Hooper in the 1950s.

county hall), had left the house to walk towards the railway station when she realised she had forgotten her handkerchief so went back to the house. If she had not gone back one of the bullets fired as the planes went over the railway station would surely have killed her. Despite the damage and the loss of life, by the next morning the hospital was up and running again as an out-patients department thanks to all the help received. In fact, by 8.30.a.m. that next day, an anonymous donor had given a generous cheque to enable the rebuilding work to start.

Jennifer Dunford tells us a lovely story concerning the infirmary many years ago. Her father, J.W.V. Sheldon (known as Jack), was houseman at the Royal Cornwall Infirmary from 1932–35. That was rather longer than it was customary to be a houseman but he had come from Bath and was very keen to work in Cornwall so he stayed at the infirmary until he obtained a job in Padstow where he went into general practice. Mrs Dunford said that he met her mother when she was working as a probationer nurse at the infirmary in 1934–35 but their courtship had to be carried out with much secrecy as the doctors and nurses were not allowed to fraternise! Not only did their friends help by passing notes between them but also the patients did their bit! Doctor Sheldon married his love in May 1935. He died rather prematurely in 1969. It is thanks to him that we have some very interesting photographs of the nurses and patients in 1934.

The City Hospital as it had become known started transferring patients to Treliske in 1992 and finally closed in February 1999.

Truro also had another source of medical help for those in need which was founded some time after the initial opening of the hospital. This was a public dispensary and the intention was to provide medical care and the medicines themselves for the needy people of Truro and the district. It was a committee that ran the charity and the members consisted of some of the local aristocracy, the Mayor of the day, a solicitor, a physician, a surgeon and about 12 others. The system was that a person in need of medical attention would contact one of the committee who would then give the sick person a letter which entitled him to six weeks' free treatment. Together with the new hospital it seemed that Truro and its environment was well provided for but, as is often the case, there were always more applicants than could be catered for and never quite enough to go around. The charity still exists today and can occasionally provide a small amount of cash to help if there is dire need.

Today, with Treliske Hospital on the outskirts of the town and all the trappings of the national health, people do not have such trouble with their health problems. The hospital seems to be growing ever bigger as new wings and departments are added and there is also the Duchy Hospital just across the road from Treliske.

Maureen Hooper with Sister Dorothy Gundry to help her receives a certificate of merit from the chief Guide.

It was not all work for the staff at the City Hospital, they had a social life as well! Seen here in 1949 are Matron Peeke and some of the staff launching the social club boat – but no casual clothes for them, it's uniform as usual. Miss Peeke was the sister of Canon C.K. Peeke of St Paul's Church and was matron for 18 years. She died aged 72 in the 1970s.

The staff of the male surgical ward at the City Hospital in 1947 come out for the camera. Left to right, back: Nurse Ninnis, Nurse Mayne, Staff Nurse Beckerleg, Sister Pope and Nurse Gundry; front: Nurse Cleary, Nurse Gillard, Nurse Bennetts and Staff Nurse Rule.

Shirley Gripe and Marjorie Parnell lark around for the children in 1954 in front of a poster of a pirate and a parrot drawn for the occasion by Marjorie's brother when he was only 15 years old.

Still with the pirate theme in this photograph – Sister Thoms, Shirley Gripe and Marge Parnell pose for the camera with other nurses and the orthopaedic sister.

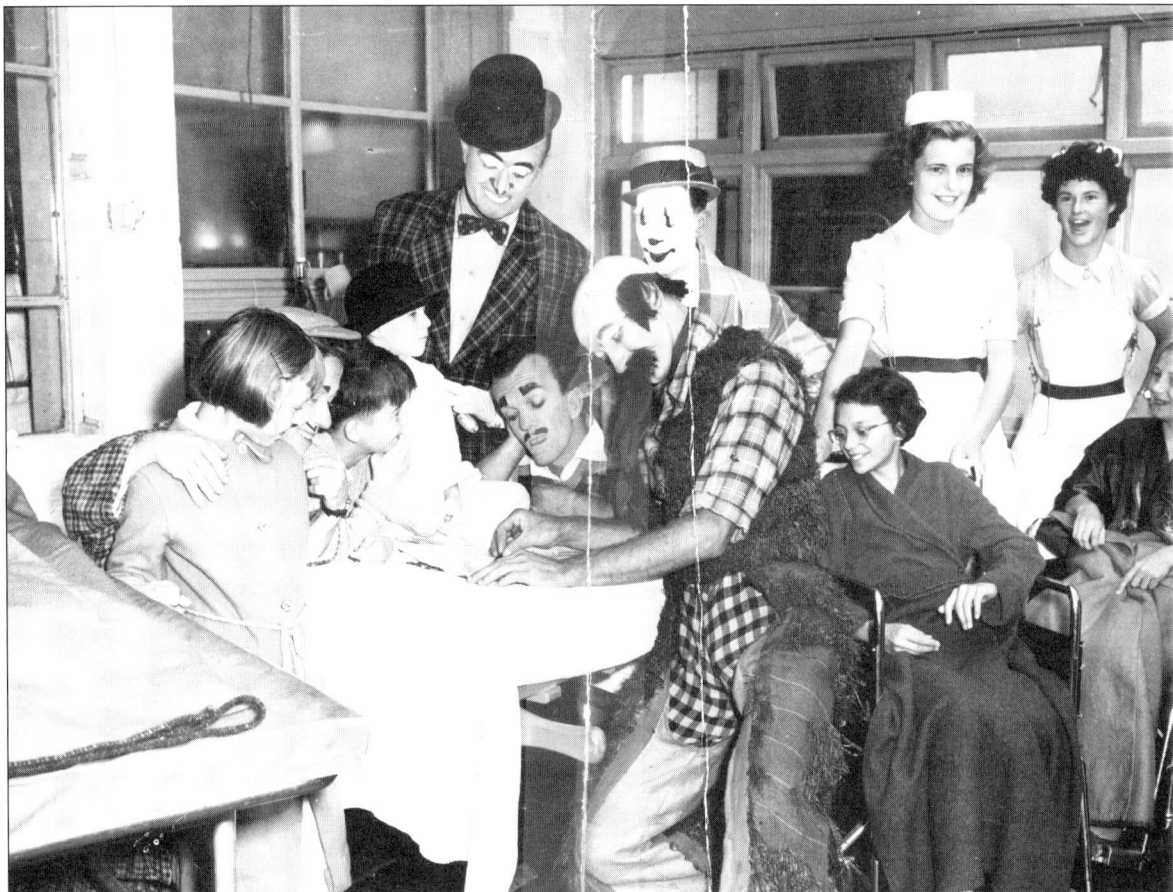

Determined to be around when there was any fun to be had, Marge Parnell and Heather Kellow make sure they are in Sister Gundry's orthopaedic ward in 1954 when the clowns from the circus came to visit. Some children were brought from Sister Tinny's ward to enjoy the occasion.

Marjorie Parnell never liked to be too serious and found time to have a chat to Jimmy the skeleton in 1953. He lived in the Preliminary Training School in Agar Road and was popped out of the window for the photo.

As well as the patients having carols sung to them to mark the festive season, the nurses had some fun too. Sister Thoms, Shirley Gripe, Marge Parnell and Catherine Birch sit down to Christmas dinner in 1955 with another nurse (bottom right) whose name unfortunately is not known. Marge said that all over the Christmas period everyone – students, nurses, doctors and even matron – tried to make it a good time for all the sad and sick people in the hospital who were worried about their families, children, etc. The nurses put on concerts and the hospital gave them lovely dinners.

During the summer of 1968 the nurses line up for Princess Alexandra at the opening of the new maternity unit known as The Princess Alexandra Maternity Ward.

Carol singing through the wards at City Hospital in 1957.

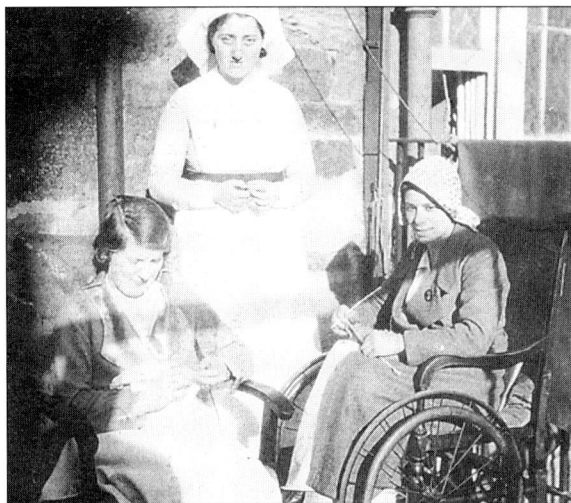

Nurse Haynes (standing), *Nurse Cuddily* (left) *and Mrs Winnie Nichols have some fresh air at the Royal Cornwall Infirmary in 1934.*

In June 1934 Dr Jack Sheldon snapped some children in the garden of the infirmary but unfortunately we do not know any of their names. The equipment looks extremely old fashioned by today's standard but the children look happy.

Chapter 8

❖

Leisure Time

The Leats outside Victoria Gardens in the early 1900s. Not only were the Waterfall Gardens and Victoria Gardens an attractive place for people to spend some leisure time but the walk through The Leats was also pleasant.

Often a service at the cathedral is preceded by a procession through the city and these members of the Royal Antediluvian Order of Buffaloes from the Joseph Oldham Gunning Lodge are making their way to a service in November 1966. Included are Dick Whitford, Dave Symons, Charlie Robins, Fred Paddy, Les Clemens and Claude Nancarrow. Behind the group it is interesting to see that the Abbey National Building Society has been in the same place for such a long time. Jays has gone and Currys has been on Garras Wharf for many years.

As the lot of the working-class people improved they found that they had leisure time to enjoy themselves. The health of the townspeople had improved immensely when Dr Clement Carlyon caused changes to be made. In 1832 there was an outbreak of cholera which, incredibly bearing in mind the open sewers which ran through the town, Truro managed to escape. Extra scavengers were employed to take away the rubbish and keep the streets clean and it seemed to work. In 1896 Dr Edward Sharp who was the medical officer of health reported that during the preceding 30 years the instances of tuberculosis had declined and he thought it was due to the fact that people were not living in such crowded conditions. However, there is no doubt that, with all the modern conveniences we have today and the standards of hygiene that we are accustomed to, we would have found their homes very unsanitary. An outside earth closet, a pump in the yard and a tin bath in front of the fire would all have been improvements in those days.

Not only did the chance of better health help the population but also the jobs available in the town would have enabled the people to earn a better living. By the latter part of the 1800s Truro had a variety of trades being carried on in its streets, among

them Beales the coach builders (established 1835), Samuel Hicks in River Street with his metalworking premises (then bicycles and later cars), and John Julian the cabinet maker and upholsterer who also acted as an undertaker and estate agent. Another cabinet maker and furnisher was the firm of Criddle and Smith, there was the family firm of the Daveys from Kea with their cooperage and Mr Joseph Pollard with his bookshop in St Nicholas Street. A.W. Jordan was another bookseller and the drapers were N. Gill and Son, Hugh Rice, and Webb and Co., and in 1903 they were joined by W.J. Roberts. W.J. Kemp and Amos Jennings were grocers, and Truro also had a steam laundry, a police force, fire brigade and a thriving railway. One could continue, but taking into account any agricultural jobs on the farms and the fact that servants were always required by the people who could afford to employ them, there were plenty of opportunities for employment even though the hours were probably long and the rewards small.

A meeting of the Royal Ancient Order of Buffaloes at the Swan Hotel in 1966 pose for the traditional photograph. These are members of the Joseph Oldham Gunning Lodge. Left to right, back row: R. Whitford, ?, R. Williams, Les Cook, ?, Claude Nancarrow, E.J. Paddy, Taff Symons, Sid Eales, ?, Les Nancarrow, H. Newton, Charles Robins; front: Charlie Davies, Alf Polmear, Hugh Brown, Les Clemens and Tommy Maunder.

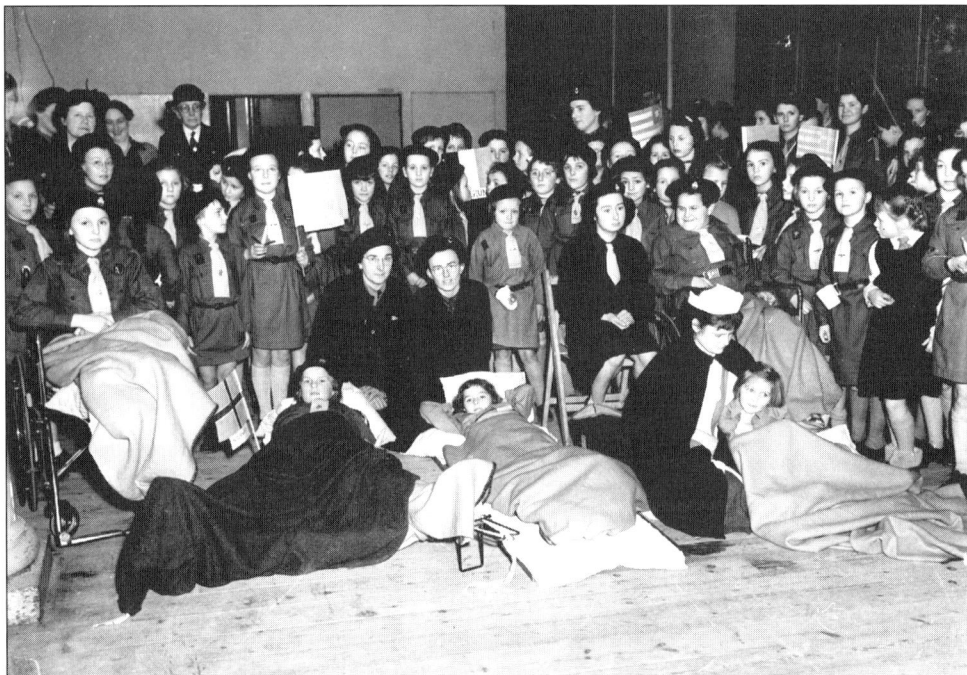

This photograph was taken for the Western Morning News *c.1955 at a gathering of Guides and Brownies in the City Hall.*

The first Truro District Rangers at Condurro in 1945 look happy as they pose with a pony. Sally Butler is the CCA and Irene Usher Region CA. An ATS sergeant is present and if one looks carefully the back view of her dog can be seen. Perhaps he did not want his photo taken!

This photo is a mystery as when John Haswell gave it to the Old Cornwall Society he had no idea who the men were or what club, society or company they represented. They are in the lane at the back of Lemon Street where today there is a service road to Gateway and the moorfield car park. Behind the group is the entrance to Beswethericks Yard. An interested onlooker is peeping out of a window on the right so perhaps this is where they came from. Who knows! Is the gentleman standing second from the right in the second row the architect Silvanus Trevail?

St Mary's Guides, Truro, c.1955, were photographed camping at Portloe. Left to right, back: *Rosemary Anstis, Marjorie Bottrill, Daphne Netten, Nina Bunney, Ann Bottrill, Jennifer Lister and Jennifer Harding;* front: *Wendy Lister, ? Meleck, Peter Bottrill, Sheila Kennedy, Pat Bawden, ? Mitchell, ?, ? Dash, Vivienne Hollow. Marjorie Bottrill could only go to the camp if she could take her son Peter with her, so that is how a little boy comes to be in the Girl Guides photo!*

It was no wonder though that with the general upturn in conditions the people of Truro looked for ways to enjoy their leisure time. The People's Palace catered for many different tastes. It was like a leisure centre combined with a working men's club and although these days there is not such a choice of activities available, it still exists. Over the years some of the activities there have included teams for skittles, a boxing club, snooker, table tennis and at one time a choir.

Sporting leisure activities in Truro included football, rugby and cricket. Truro City Football Club was reputedly founded in 1889 and later, together with seven other clubs, formed the Cornwall County Association. Playing in red and black, 'Up the City' was always a familiar call from the supporters.

Truro Rugby Club struggled after the First World War, although in the 1920s it was revived and a junior club was formed. As for cricket it is thought that it was in 1810 that the Truro Cricket Club was born. By 1900 they were playing at Tremorvah and Mr Chellew, the eccentric ship owner, was their patron. Cricket ceased for the duration of the war and when it resumed Mr Chellew no longer allowed them to play on his land and just to make sure that they did not, he built a wall across the pitch! There must have

been a falling out about something! Until 1959 the club used the pitch of the Truro City Football Club in Treyew Road but then they leased from the city council what is still today the cricket club ground. It had been the dump at the end of Boscawen Park and in effect is reclaimed land. With careful and loving attention it was transformed into a good pitch in attractive grounds.

The ladies also had their societies and one was the Women's Institute which was formed in Truro in 1918 with 100 members and went from strength to strength. In 1919 the Cornwall Federation of Women's Institutes was formed and Mrs Harcourt Williams of Truro became the first county chairman.

Old Cornwall Societies first appeared in the 1920s and Truro was the second town to form its own society. It had become obvious to many Cornish scholars and those interested in their local heritage throughout the county that so many newcomers were arriving in the county to live and work that things were changing forever. The local dialects were fast disappearing, as was the folklore and the remains of the language. People's jobs were changing, the way the Cornish lived and worked all underwent changes and so the local history societies were born. The motto of the Federation of Old Cornwall

The Boys Club have turned out for a football match c.1969 and the Mayor, Arnold Hodge, has attended.

The proud snooker players who have won trophies were players from the People's Palace. Photographed c.1950, they are Brian Pascoe, Ron Cowling, Brian Lord and George Champion with Dennis Mitchell seated in the middle.

The People's Palace had many different clubs within its walls and one of them was the Truro Skittles Club. This photograph is c.1900 and at this distance of time unfortunately only one person can be named. Seated in the front row with the impressive moustache and the highly polished boots is Francis Minto Benny aged approximately 26. He married Annie Kemp, the maidservant to the Kendall family, and their elder daughter Freda Young attained the age of 90 on 24 November 2003.

This is the first match played on the new cricket ground at Boscawen Park on 12 May 1961. Left to right, standing: Jack Angove (Troon), Peter Barnicoat (Truro), Ivan Hine (Falmouth), Peter Marriott (Truro), Tom Meneer (Falmouth), Tony Rodda (Redruth), Ivor Skinner (Falmouth), Dennis Triniman (Redruth), Alan Eulo (Truro), Ralph Dorning (Falmouth), Ron Tither (Truro), Jimmy Vincent (Troon), Colin Taylor (Truro), Len Chapman (Truro), Arnold Powning (Truro), Peter Hoggett (Truro), Ray Stephens (Truro), Richard James (Truro); seated: Ray Roberts (Truro), Martin Tobin (Redruth), Captain T.W.R. Christophers (chairman, Truro), Viv Percy (captain, Truro), Noel Dorning (Falmouth), R.L. Frank (president, Truro), Frank Manning (Truro), John Warne (Truro).

Truro Bowling Club have beautiful grounds in Kenwyn Road. This is a shot of their old clubhouse just before it was demolished.

On a bright summer day the bowlers enjoy a game outside their new clubhouse at Truro Bowling Club. The new building was erected in 1992.

As well as work these staff of the West Briton *got to play as they were the cricket team. They are seen here in the early 1950s. Left to right, back row: Pat Loze, Bob Prowse, Trevor Thomas, Reggie Loze, Barry Bennetts, Horace Churm, Brian Pascoe, Mike Trevail, Ron Hill; front: Gerry Clarke, Cresby Nicholas and Charlie Street.*

Canon Ken Rogers (known as Father Ken), the President of Truro Old Cornwall Society 2000 and 2001, addresses the members at their Christmas lunch at the Carlton Hotel. Left to right: Christine Parnell, honorary secretary, Arthur Lyne, honorary life member, past president and past secretary of 40 years, Father Ken and Ethelwyn Parker. Mrs Parker, a language bard, always says grace in Cornish and arranges the meal each Christmas.

The winners of the County Team Championship posed with their trophy at Truro Golf Club in 1981. Left to right, back: Peter Kneebone, Nick Cocking, Andrew Morton, Andrew Knuckey, Graham Stephens, David Kneebone, Dick Perkins; front: Marc Boggia, Ray Shirley (South West President), John Rich (captain), Andrew Ring, Mike Roberts.

A large crowd of members of the Women's Gas Federation attend a cookery demonstration in the gas showrooms in Boscawen Street, c.1920. Even if many of the ladies present did not have the very latest in gas cookers they would have hoped one day to have one and any ideas for new recipes would have been very welcome.

This is a Royal Naval Association parade on Back Quay but the year is uncertain. Those who know them will be able to pick out Fred Albon, Tom Martin and Tommy Maunder.

Societies is 'gather up the fragments that nothing be lost' and the most important person in any society is the recorder who can keep (hopefully) a record of his area and gather up any artefacts that will help those in the future to remember and understand the history of the town. The Truro society was formed on 15 June 1922 and celebrated its 80th birthday with a dinner at the Carlton Hotel on 15 June 2002 where Mrs Joy Stevenson entertained members with her amusing dialect stories after the meal.

Arnold Hodge and Peter Parnell examine some old photographs of Truro while waiting for the Truro Old Cornwall Society's Christmas Lunch at the Carlton Hotel in 2001.

January 2004 was the 50th anniversary of the formation of the Townswomen's Guild but it also saw their last meeting. They decided to disband as they were finding it difficult to attract younger members and the current ladies had decided that they had had enough of being on the committee and doing all the organising themselves with no others coming along behind them ready to take office in the future. A photograph in the *West Briton* of some of the ladies with a beautiful cake ready to be cut marked the end of an era for them.

The year 1961 saw the formation of the Truro Civic Society with the aim of encouraging:

... high standards of architecture and town planning in the City and to stimulate public interest in the care of the beauty, history and character of the City and its surroundings.

The first chairman was the Mayor, Mr S.J. Sunley, and the secretary was Mr John Crowther. In 1977, the year of the Queen's silver jubilee, one of the Civic Society's schemes was the redecoration of the city centre. Another excellent offshoot of the society was the formation of the Truro Buildings Group which has done much to record the history and use of many of the city's properties. Their distinctive black and white covered books are much sought after and valued by anyone interested in the history of Truro.

Truro had had a cinema since 1912 known as The Regent situated in the City Hall. For many years there was another form of entertainment in the City Hall – an ice rink. In 1921 the Palace Cinema opened for business and The Plaza in Lemon Street was built in the early 1930s as its architecture suggests. The Hall for Cornwall at the back of the Municipal Buildings (or the building known as the City Hall) is a popular source of entertainment these days with a great variety of stage productions. When a Russian company staged an ice spectacular about Barnum and his circus not long before this volume was written, it was the first time for many years that an ice rink had been seen in Truro.

This is part of the display of kitchen equipment in the gas showrooms, probably in the 1920s, and shows a cooker, a stove and on the other side of a wall not too close to the heat the very latest in fridges (all gas of course).

A gas cooker has been used to make this cake and a selection of buns all within the setting of a modern kitchen in the gas showrooms. The room next to it is a dining-room or perhaps a lounge (usually known in Truro as a front room whether it was in the front of a house or not) and it would almost certainly have featured a gas fire.

Not enough names are known but perhaps people will recognise themselves when looking at this picture. It is a Christmas party for the children of those employed in the fire brigade c.1969. Debbie and Lindsay Allam are in the photo and Father Christmas is Tony Jennings.

A production of Carousel *in the City Hall is captured here with the players waiting backstage. Left to right: Margaret Salmon, Jennifer Powell, Jennifer Penna, Chris Collins, ?, Rosemary Anstis, Rosemary Alsept.*

This Robert Roskrow photo was taken in 1978 of the Truro Amateur Operatic Society Junior Showtime. Left to right, back: *Suzanne Thomas, Rebecca Watson, Mandy Penhaligon, Joanna Rowe, Debbie Gilbert, Lisa Price, Kerenza Jago, Rachel Grose;* front: *Lyn Carveth, Ian Price, Christopher Jago, Claire Harding, Claire Thomas, Helen Gilbert, Georgina Beeching, Sarah Willis, Debbie Rowe, Trudie Reeves.*

Truro Amateur Operatic Dramatic Society (TAODS) have put on many shows over the years. In 1979 members of the junior showtime gave a performance on a stage decorated with flowers. Left to right: *Mandy Penhaligon, Lyn Carveth, Claire Harding, Joanna Rowe, Deborah Gilbert and Lisa Price.*

The amateur operatic dramatic society performed White Horse Inn *in 1965 and from left to right we see David Buzza, John Colston and Geoff Carveth.*

In 1966 TAODS gave a performance of Vagabond King. *On the left is Kenwin Barton as the Herald of Burgundy and Geoff Carveth on the right. Kenwin Barton was famed for his musical abilities and regularly sang with the police choir and also performed many Gilbert and Sullivan works.*

Although the cast of a production in any dramatic society is important and people are remembered for the part they played and the performance they gave, many other people would have contributed to make the performance a success. In this photograph of 1960 we see the programme sellers for the Truro Opera. Included in the picture are Barbara Martin (née Phillips), Marjorie Woodland, Jill Ratcliffe and Mrs Lampier.

Chapter 9

❖

Wartime Memories

We have already read of the wartime memories of Sybil Rapsey and Dennis Mitchell as they recalled the bombs dropping on the hospital but of course so many people remember different things that it would be impossible to record them all.

Marlene Ellis (now Pond) recalls that the bombs were dropped on a Saturday as it was on a Saturday that the family had their treat of fish and chips. Her

Not everyone who went away to war came back in triumph as this picture tells us. They are members of the Royal Garrison Artillery heavy Howitzer gun crew during the First World War. After the second Battle of the Somme, the only survivor was Corporal Edwin John Paddy of Truro, shown here seated in the front.

mother Christine Pearl Ellis and father Roland James Ellis (known as Jim) were with her and they all had to take cover as they queued for the meal. Everyone in the shop was terrified as they all realised what would happen to the hot fat in the fryer if the bombs hit them and it was only later that they heard about the crater the bombs had caused at the hospital.

Russell Martin recalls that he and his brother were the first two men called up who were in reserved occupations, both of them being farmers at Killiow. They got through the war safely but on his return to the farm, Russell's brother was killed when he entered one of the barns and a stray bomb that no one realised was there exploded. He was only 24.

Jon Summers – whose father Norman ran the 'seed shop' as many people thought of it – has a very interesting tale to tell. It was not until many years after the war that the whole story came out and then he was amazed. At the time, the family lived in Chapel Hill and behind their house backing on to Mutton's field were some garages. As everyone had to think of safety, Mr Summers decided that he would dig back through a garage into the field that rose above it and create an Anderson shelter for his family. The shelter was regularly used, but on one particular occasion, when the siren sounded and the whole family trooped out to the shelter, Mr Summers refused to go inside. Everyone else seated themselves as comfortably as possible on a large wooden box that had been recently put there but Father paced up and down outside and no amount of cajoling from Mrs Summers would get him inside.

Many years later Jon discovered that his father, who they all knew had been in the Home Guard, was in fact in the secret army (whose headquarters were in the old Wheal Jane). It turned out that the box on which the family had settled themselves was in fact full of high explosives and on its way to Wheal Jane for use should Cornwall be invaded! Fortunately no bombs dropped that night, but it would have been a 'bombshell' if Mr Summers had had to divulge that to his family!

Music has always been important in the lives of the Cornish and the Duke of Cornwall's Light Infantry Brass Band would undoubtedly have played for many a march and ceremonial occasion. The Truro band c.1902 are now largely unknown but bandsman Edwin James Paddy is on the far right of the middle row.

Bandsman Edwin James Paddy is seated middle row fourth from the left in this 1892 photograph of the Band of 12th Company 1st Cornwall Duke of Cornwall's Royal Garrison Artillery Volunteers.

This is a photograph of the Ponsford family during the First World War. Back left is Jack with Alice beside him. Ethel and Phyllis are in the middle row and Meta and Audrey are in front. Their father who had 13 children volunteered for service and was sent to the Dardenelles with other volunteers who were all in their forties. Sadly they all drowned and never returned to their families.

Winnie Crago's father Henry Charles Carpenter poses in his First World War uniform. He survived the war although a brother of his was killed. Yet another brother was famous in his family for having shares in The Scillonian, the steamship which plied between Penzance and the Isles of Scilly. The family lived at 6 Fairmantle Street and Henry was in charge of the Working Men's Club in Lemon Street.

Members of the Royal Navy Association parade on Back Quay, c.1960. Included in the photo are J. Davey, Jock Milne, Bob Hay, Fred Albon and, head and shoulders above the others and wearing a black hat, Captain Pollard.

Miss Ada Alvey was a well-known person in Truro for several reasons. In 1955 she had given up her position as Honorary Secretary of the Truro Old Cornwall Society due to work commitments. She was a teacher of geography at Truro County Grammar School for Girls and also taught handwriting to the new intake each year. In order to write legibly and quickly all the pupils were taught to write plainly using an italic nib and even to this day old girls can be spotted by their style of handwriting. Although she taught girls, Ada loved the boys as well and devoted many years to running her group of Cubs. Before her death, she was often to be found enjoying a cup of coffee in the cathedral's coffee shop and one day the author joined her and got talking. She related the tale about the elephant she had adopted and how delighted she was to be able to do something positive to help the wildlife of the world. She also had a fascinating tale to tell about the war.

In 1971 the Royal British Legion celebrated its 50th anniversary and Truro City Parks Department did them proud with a floral display in Victoria Gardens. Shown from the left are R.J. Williams, K.J. Tonkin, Bill Jewell, club chairman, Gerry Mitchell, Anthony Barber, Mayor, George Bond, R. Whitford, Mervyn Steeds (head of the Parks Department) and Bill Udy.

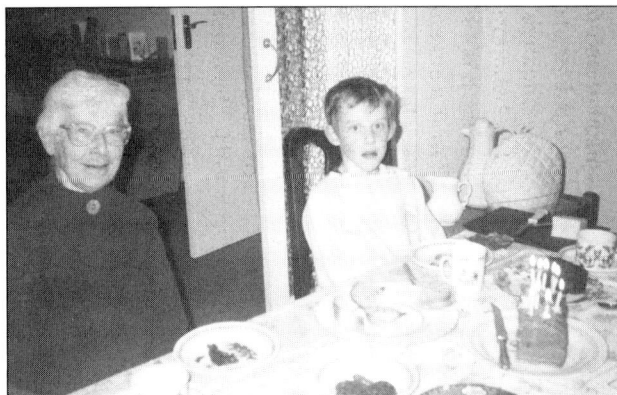

Miss Alvey is seen at a birthday celebration at the home of Mrs Griffin many years after she had her experience in Spandau!

In 1939 she and her sister went to Germany to have a holiday, staying in youth hostels and lodgings and cycling from place to place. One night, wanting to send some postcards home and not having any stamps, she went out to buy some, not realising that there was a curfew and that she should not be out. When she was tapped on the shoulder she turned to be confronted by a very handsome young man in the uniform of a German officer who asked her why she was out and what she was doing. She explained about the stamps and he told her to go with him. He led her to a castle where guards jumped to attention as they entered and they went into a room where he gave her the stamps for her postcards. They then left the castle and he escorted her to the postbox. Finally he took her back to her lodgings and told her not to venture out after curfew again. It was only a day or two before the sisters

Bill Carpenter spent his war in North Africa. He volunteered for the Services and drove a lorry during the war as his peace-time job was to drive for Spillers Flour. While he was away Miss Bennetts the hairdresser helped his wife with the three children. When he came home, as Spillers would not pay any overtime, he went to work for Regent Petrol as a lorry driver. He died in 1993.

Bill Carpenter with his lorry. He made a mistake during the war which saved his life. His orders were to drive onto a landing craft but he mistook where he was supposed to go and drove onto the wrong one. The landing craft he should have been on was blown up and all those aboard died; this was a lucky escape for him but it was a very traumatic experience seeing all his mates killed.

Truro's Jack Pascoe joined the RAF and served in Iceland during the Second World War. Many people will remember his family for their excellent fish and chip shop.

decided that things were serious in Europe – that the war which they thought would never happen was imminent and so they returned home. Safely back at home before war was declared, the girls avidly read the newspapers to keep abreast of the news. It was their custom to take turns in having a lie-in on a Sunday morning and just a week or two after the outbreak of war Ada's sister brought the Sunday paper and a cup of tea to her in bed. The picture on the front page was a castle and Ada realised with a shock that it was the same one into which she had gone for her stamps. Suddenly she realised that she had been in Spandau and much later knew that she was possibly the only English person for many years to leave the castle alive.

The blacksmiths in Kenwyn Street, Fred Mitchell senr and son Byryn, had an amusing tale to tell. At this time Fred junr was away in the Army but the other two were in the Home Guard as their job was classed as a reserved occupation. They always had horses to shoe and agricultural implements to mend –

The Dreadnought playing fields at Hendra were used during the war to parade troops. A special police constable, possibly Frank Tremelling, stands at ease watching them.

Fred Mitchell and his son Byryn were in reserved occupations and so were in the Home Guard. Being blacksmiths and farriers, their skills were needed to keep the farmers' tools in good repair and in fact they could turn their hands to most things. Fred had done his bit in the First World War and was gassed at Ypres.

even car springs could be welded and fixed back on the vehicle (if anyone could get the petrol to make it worthwhile having a car). A public information film had been shown in the town, with some beautifully spoken people exhorting the farmers not to waste anything, nor to look to buy new tools but to make do and mend. One of the things the film suggested was that the farmers looked out their old harrows for ploughing and several worried men came into the smithy saying that they had never had any harrows and did not even know what they were. "Arras boys, arras", said Fred in his Cornish accent, and daylight broke across the faces of the farmers. Of course they had 'arras' and they knew exactly where to find them and how to put them to good use!

Some families were split apart for most of the war and one of those was the Teague family of Hendra. Father, Bill, had served in the First World War for three and a half years and was wounded and reported missing whilst fighting the Turks. In the Second World War he was in the Home Guard and also on fire-watching duties. His eldest son Reg joined the Royal Engineers in the early part of 1940 and served in Iceland for two years. Later he was to serve in North Africa and it was from there that he took part in the invasion of Sicily. His sister tells us that he was transferred to the 56th division of the battle for Italy where amongst other duties he had to search for land mines and build bridges. He was demobbed in Triest in Yugoslavia in 1946 and made it home safely. The second son of the family was Arthur who enlisted in the RAF in 1941

and after moving around RAF stations in England and Scotland was sent to the Orkney Islands and then to the Pacific. Finally he went to Hong Kong and Kowloon where he guarded Japanese prisoners of war. He was also demobbed in 1946. The third son, Ronald, had been in the ATC as a schoolboy then joined the RAF aged 18 at Christmas 1942. Because of all the terrible losses at sea there was a call for people to transfer to the Royal Navy and that was what Ron did. He was transferred to the Indian Ocean and like his brothers was demobbed in 1946. The youngest son Cyril joined the Royal Navy aged 18 in 1944 and he was also sent to the Indian Ocean where he served on the aircraft carrier HMS *Victorious*. He was demobbed in 1946.

Mrs Teague died in 1942 not knowing that her sons were all to return home safely from the war, but she also did her bit. As the family home was just a stone's throw from the Hendra drill hall, she used to carefully put out a flask of tea and a flask of coffee every night under the bushes by her garden wall so that the soldiers on patrol could have a hot drink. All she hoped was that somewhere someone was doing a kindness for one of her boys.

Because her mother had died, Joyce, the elder daughter, was made exempt from call up so that she could look after her father and young brother. Not wanting to be left out of the war effort, however, she became a member of the Royal Observer Corps. Her younger sister Doreen joined the WAAF in 1942 and she also had to go away and serve on various stations in England and Wales. She was also demobbed in 1946 and none of the family had any opportunity to return home until their demobilisation.

Geoff Carveth has some memories of the Americans who were stationed in Cornwall. On summer evenings at about six o'clock he would be sent down to meet his father who worked in the fuel depot at Malpas. The Americans who were stationed at Tolverne often came over to Malpas at about this time as some of the officers liked to go to the pub for a drink and their subordinates had orders to collect them at a certain time. Quite often Geoff and his father would be hidden on their boat by the Americans and taken back to Tolverne for the evening where his father would be allowed to go ashore for a drink but Geoff had to remain hidden on the boat. This was no hardship for Geoff, however, as he was given a supply of sweets, chewing gum, oranges and bananas to keep him happy – all exciting things which were not available here in wartime and guaranteed to appeal to a young boy with a healthy appetite.

Arthur Teague is seen here when he was in Hong Kong, or maybe Kowloon where he guarded Japanese prisoners of war.

Bill Teague of Hendra saw all of his family off to war except his daughter Joyce. He was well known in Truro as he drove the motorised Truro Steam Laundry van for many years.

Above: *Taken on 19 October 1941, this picture shows Ronald Teague on the left with his pal Douglas Hodge.*

Left: *Reg Teague worked for Tregunna the builders and undertakers as a mason and plasterer after the war.*

Cyril Teague sent this photograph of himself home to 'Dad and Joyce with love'.

Joyce Teague who stayed at home to 'keep the home fires burning' in her Royal Observer Corps uniform.

Doreen Teague who worked as an accountant at H.E. Bowden and Co. and for Lang Bennetts after the war.

Four Truro men take time out to pose in the early 1940s. Back left is Donald Thomas, later a barber in Victoria Square, and beside him is Ken Launder who was later a printer at Jordan's in Boscawen Street. Front left is Ron Launder who worked as a carpenter for Parkins in St Clement Street after the war and beside him is Bill Chappel who worked at Fyffes banana stores. Joan Launder tells us that the only one still alive is Donald Thomas as Bill Chappel died a few years ago, her husband Ken died in April 2003 and his brother two years before that. She and Ken had been married for 63 years.

Joyce Teague believes this Royal Observer Corps group was photographed in 1943 outside the pavilion at the Rugby Football Club in St Clement's Hill before moving to the Masonic Hall but Arthur Lyne, a founder member of the corps, says that it was the Truro School pavilion. This was used temporarily as they usually met in the Masonic Hall. Left to right, back row: *Mr Opie, Doris Williams, Mr H. Pearce, Mr Tiffany, Harry Clements, Mr G. Pearce, Miss Thomson, Mr Jones;* middle row: *Mr Bradley, Mr Sawle, Jim Drewett, Mr Balme, Mr W. Pearce, Mr White, Mr L. Roberts, Mr S. Roberts, Mr Webb;* front: *Pat Brown, Mrs De Vescovi, Eileen Pryor and Joyce Teague.*

Mrs Phil Smith (who with her husband worked for about 25 years in their grocery shop in New Bridge Street until her son and his wife took over) remembers her sister who had a distinguished career in the WRAF. Joyce Borlase went to the County Grammar School for Girls then attended the Truro Diocesan Training College for Teachers and then moved on to the Physical Training College in London. After all that, she announced that she was going to join the WRAF, which she did in October 1941. Although she joined as an aircraftswoman, she became a squadron officer and in 1950, aged 32, she was awarded an MBE in the New Year Honours List. In 1946–47 she had taken the first group of women in the Air Force to America and photographs in her album not only show her sitting behind her own desk with her name plate in front of her looking very happy but also exploring the wonders of America.

It is not only the Second World War which took people away from the town. Truro's Mike Rowe

had a peaceful existence as the manager of Halfords and combined it with being a Territorial Army captain. Although he had been in the Territorial Army for 35 years he had never been mobilised until January 2003 when he was given one week's notice that his services were required. He was sent to Marchwood near Southampton with 165 Regiment (Volunteers), where for long hours, seven days a week for eight weeks, ships destined for the Gulf were loaded and made ready. When all the ships had left Mike and his regiment had several weeks of training still to be completed before being sent to the Gulf themselves in May. They took control of two ports and ran them successfully before being posted back to Marchwood two and a half months later. Mike was the only Cornishman in the regiment and felt proud of the way they did their duty. A year later, however, he is back in his shop and very relieved that he is safely home – a sentiment shared by his wife Sharman.

Above: *Sidney W. Hancock, a Perranporth boy, served in the Eighth Army during the North Africa campaign and is seen here on the right. He is in a dug-out in the Libyan desert in 1942 with his pal G.E. Shergold of Sutton, Warminster, Wiltshire.*

Left: *Joyce Borlase who was awarded the MBE in the New Year's Honours List 1950.*

The Royal Observer Corps are outside a sports pavilion which looks as though it is at Truro School. Unfortunately only a few names can be recalled. Left to right, back row: ?, ?, Alfred S. Mansell, ?, ?, John Paddy, ?, J.C. Greener; front: James Finn, ?, ?, Griffith Sandy, ?, Gordon L. Grose, ?, Frank Lewis, ?.

Chapter 10

❖

Civic Life

Over the years Truro has had many city councillors, some of whom have gone on to become the Mayor. In the local government reorganisation of 1974 the nature of the city council changed as most of its powers were taken away by the new district council and whereas at one time the city councillors were responsible for much of the business involved in running the town, this was lost to them.

In 1965, a young butcher called Arnold Hodge was busy building his new business into a thriving concern when Councillor Mrs Elsie Cornish called on him to ask him to stand for the city council. Mr Hodge was already a Chacewater parish councillor as he used to live there, and he had been on their council for 17 years. The business he had recently taken over was run down and he needed to put a lot of effort into it to support his family, so he hesitated to add more work to his already busy schedule. Seeing that he was not too keen, Mrs Cornish went to fetch the application papers for him and took them up to his shop. Stressing the fact that she was an old woman and she had walked all the way to the town hall to get the papers and all the way back again she more or less obliged him to fill them in and return them! When his nomination was received two ladies who had applied both withdrew and Mr Hodge joined the city council unopposed, the only time in his subsequently long career in politics that such an event occurred.

The Mayor's secretary, Jack Manuell, required him to attend at the town hall on a Thursday afternoon at 2p.m. to sign the declaration, and in no time at all he had become Councillor Hodge.

Mayor making was a rigid tradition and all the councillors had to assemble in the upstairs lobby outside the town hall which was also used as the magistrates court where the ceremony was to take place. The town clerk was called Harold Thomas and according to Mr Hodge he had a watch as big as a frying pan which he had previously put right with the town clock. The councillors were lined up, half outside one door and the other half outside the opposite door

In 1969–70 the Mayor, Arnold Hodge, and Mayoress Violet Hodge are shown an antique by Arthur Negus, star of many television antiques programmes, while Mrs Smith looks on.

and as Mr Thomas watched the time the tension would mount. At the first strike of the town clock he would say 'We're moving' and by the time it had struck 12, all the councillors would be in the room on either side of the Mayor. The ceremony had to last until one o'clock when the new Mayor, officers and guests were expected at the Royal Hotel for lunch.

When it was his turn to be Mayor (1969–70) Arnold Hodge knew what to expect as he had seen it all so many times before. The treasurer, Lewis Nicholls (who had been a prisoner of war held by the Japanese), wrote half his speech for him and he had to write the second half himself and make it last until one o'clock! He reported on progress in the sewerage extensions in Highertown which would make available more land for housing, he spoke of planned work in the High Cross area and of the modernisation of the cattle market, amongst other things. Present at the Mayor making was Mr R.R. Blewett who had been Arnold's schoolmaster at St Day. Mr Blewett was 88 years old and had been awarded his MA degree the year before at the age of 87!

As the new Mayor, Mr Hodge invested the outgoing Mayor Kingsley Smith as his Deputy

The Mayor of 2001, John Fletcher Peters, takes the salute as the Royal British Legion march through Boscawen Street.

In 1985–6 the Mayor, the Reverend Douglas Robins, speaks to the people of Truro outside the Municipal Buildings. As 1985 saw the 700th anniversary of one of the charters granted to Truro there were festivities throughout the town. The mace bearers are Mr Carpenter on the left with John Cockle behind him and Mr Eva on the right with the town clerk Ray Reynolds at the back.

Mayor, and the new Mayoress, Mrs Violet Hodge, invested Mrs Smith as the Deputy Mayoress. These days things are done differently, the Deputy Mayor becoming the Mayor the following year.

The Mayoress' 'at home' attracted guests from all over town in such numbers that there was a queue from the town hall, down all the steps to the street and stretching back around the corner of Lower Lemon Street that is around London House, which at that time housed W.H. Smith the bookseller. The Hodges had hired outside caterers to do the tea, Mr and Mrs Bailey of the Brookdale Hotel. The mayoral allowance at that time was £500, half of which was paid before the Mayor choosing (in May) and the rest had to be applied for in November. Mr Nicholls would never dream of parting with the city's money without being asked and it was only the intervention of Alderman Arthur Behenna who insisted that Mr Hodge should have his money and went with him to personally make sure he received it, that it was paid at all. The Mayor was glad of it as in those days he even had to buy all the Christmas cards out of his allowance or his own pocket and every old age pensioner received a card from the Mayor and Mayoress!

The second engagement of his mayoralty was to open and welcome the Diocesan Conference in the chapter house of the cathedral. The bishop, Dr Key and a canon were waiting for him to escort him into the chapter house where he was alarmed to see vicars seated all around. The bishop asked him why he did not seem comfortable and he explained that he felt nervous having to address a roomful of professional public speakers. 'Don't worry about that' said the bishop, 'You will only have been on your feet for five minutes and they will all be sleeping!' Just the week before the Mayor had had trouble during a council meeting with a couple of councillors and he had warned them to abide by standing orders or he would adjourn the meeting, which news had been gleefully reported in the paper for all to read. When the bishop introduced the Mayor to the conference he told them 'If we have any nonsense and you don't go to sleep he will rule you out of order!'

The Friends of the Royal Cornwall Hospital used to have their AGM in the lecture theatre at the old city hospital and the Mayor of the city was always invited to move the accounts. Miss Johnstone of Trewithen was the Chairman and Lady Falmouth the President and when he was requested to attend, an appointments form was sent out by his secretary so that their requirements would be known to the Mayor. He was assured that he would be met and that there would be somewhere for him to park but

there was no request for him to wear the mayoral chain of office. On arrival Miss Johnstone showed him into an ante room so that he could don the chain and was surprised to find that he had not brought it. Lady Falmouth confessed that she had not asked for it as she believed there was a fee of £5 for him to wear it and she did not want to waste their funds. She was wrong, there was no fee, but the mistake enabled the Mayor to compliment her in his speech as he pointed out that every penny of their hard-earned cash was spent on the things that mattered and nothing was wasted, and he assured them that there was no fee for the Mayor to wear the chain of office and that next year he would see to it that the Mayor wore the chain.

In 1930, someone called Trewin in New Zealand died and left a legacy to the Mayor of Truro to be spent on the poor at Christmas. Mr Hodge found that during his mayoral year the interest from the legacy (sent from New Zealand each year) amounted to £300 and it was his decision how the money was to be spent. The advice he was given by Alderman Behenna was not to give money but to buy something to give to the people and to keep a record of how the money was spent. It was a heavy responsibility but the decision he came to benefited more than just the poor. At the beginning of Christmas week he went into the Furniss factory and said, 'I want £300 of biscuits as soon as possible!' This meant that all the staff who had been laid off after the summer rush had a week's work and all in all the managers at the factory were delighted to produce boxes with three kinds of biscuits in each. Mr Freddy Marsh in charge of public health and housing was able to supply a list of council-house tenants who were considered to be needy and the plan was to distribute the boxes of biscuits before Christmas. Mrs Hodge and Barbara Salmon who worked for her could not believe the state of the Hodges' long and high hallway after the biscuits had been delivered; they were stacked up to the ceiling all the length of the hall! To start with they were wrapping the boxes before delivery but they ran out of paper, energy and time! One night after work when the Mayor was trying to find his way around the estate at Trelander to deliver the parcels he decided to knock at the door of Mr Sid Tann to ask for directions. He came to the door stripped to the waist, wearing no shirt and no vest and found a harassed Mayor who explained what he was trying to do. 'The car is stacked right up with them Sid and I don't know where I'm going.' Without bothering to stop to put a jacket on Mr Tann set off to help the Mayor with his load of boxes and before long they were all delivered. The Mayor was delighted with his helper and Sid was pleased that it

Mr Kingsley Smith and Mrs Smith are dressed in costume in High Cross in 1985–6, the occasion being the same one as the photograph with the Reverend Douglas Robins on the podium celebrating 700 years since the charter granted to Truro by Edward I. Richard De Lucy had granted privileges to the town in 1140 and the earliest existing charter granted by Reginald Earl of Cornwall between 1161 and 1166 confirmed these privileges. Earl Reginald's charter was confirmed by one of Henry II's which no longer exists and the Charter of Edward I dated 12 June 1285 was the cause of the 700-year celebrations.

A mayoral procession wends its way through Boscawen Street. They have probably attended a service at the cathedral and are making their way back to the Municipal Buildings. The Mayor is Alderman William Arthur Phillips (Mayor 1919–20). He is the grandfather of Barbara Martin and Desmond Phillips.

Truro City Councillors gather outside the Municipal Buildings. Behind them is the advertisement for the Regent Cinema which was housed in the same building. Left to right, back row: A.A. Behenna, J.R. Behenna and A. Phillips; front: ?, ?, ?, Horace Cornish, Mr Fillbrook, Mr Teague, ?, C. Wright, ?, ?. This photograph was taken in the 1950s.

was his knowledge that had got the job done. For years after whenever they met Sid said to Arnold, 'We put out the parcels!', and Arnold knew he could not have done it without him.

Although it was very hard work Mr Hodge would do it all again and as well as the prestige of being a past Mayor of Truro he has had other accolades. In 1987 on 5 January he was given the freedom of the city of Truro and in 1988 he was made a Bard of the Cornish Gorsedd. Another honour came his way when he was given the freedom of the city of London on 4 November 1997. He has also met many members of the royal family over the years and had some very interesting engagements.

Mr Clifford Tidball, who used to work for the *West Briton*, was posted to Cardiff where he became the sports commentator for the radio. He became the President of the Cardiff Cornish Association during Mr Hodge's mayoral year and invited him to be the guest speaker at their annual dinner. The Mayor went and was met at Newport and taken to see the rugby at Cardiff Arms Park in the press box. Then, at the request of a long-serving member of the Cardiff Cornish Association, originally a Hayle man, he was taken to that gentleman's house to change into his robes before going to the dinner at the Leofric Hotel. Violet had to stay at home to run the shop and look after their son David but she need not have worried that her husband might miss his meals. The dining table at the old man's house was all laid out in grand style and when they had eaten he saw Arnold off in a Rolls Royce that he had hired especially and insisted that the Mayor sat in the front so that the people of Cardiff could see the chain of office. Unfortunately the old man's name has been forgotten and he was too old to attend himself for the evening dinner. Clifford Tidball proposed a toast to the City of Truro and the Mayor replied – then came a surprise; at midnight the party danced the conga in the main street led by the dance band! The Mayor of Helston turned up uninvited but he was a Welshman and was made welcome.

A Methodist minister, Mr Bunney from Camborne, was present at this dinner and he

In 1977 Miss Ena Coombe was the Mayor and her sister was her consort. They are seen here with the town crier beside the war memorial. Miss Coombe was known to many as 'Skipper' as she ran a group of Sea Rangers who were often to be seen rowing up and down the river at Malpas.

suggested that as he was the secretary of the London Cornish Association and their annual dinner was to be held in a fortnight's time the Mayor of Truro might also like to attend that one. Mr Hodge said that if he was free he would be delighted but privately decided that he could not leave his family and his business again so soon and so he would be otherwise engaged when the invitation came. Mr Bunney outmanoeuvred him, however, by asking the Mayor's secretary Des Hoskin if the Mayor was engaged on that particular date, and on being assured that he was not, Mr Bunney said that the Mayor had said he would go to London if he was free to do so and so Arnold found himself booked for another posh dinner, this time in London where Lord Foote was the dinner chairman and one of the members was Leonard Thomas, a former director of South Crofty and the director of a bank in London. Apparently it was another enjoyable occasion, but not as good as Cardiff as there was no conga!

that it was water for which the city council was responsible that was flooding this property and so Mr Wilson had the water turned off. This in turn led to complaints to the councillors from people who liked to see the water from the leats running through the town and so at a finance committee meeting the subject was brought up. This was an ongoing problem for several years and when £50 was allowed to be used to pay for the repairs, Councillor Hodge said that it could not be done with such a small amount of cash and if they did not intend to fix it, they were to let him know and he would tell the people who wanted their water back that it would not happen. Actually he was about to prove himself wrong. Alderman Behenna moved that £500 be set aside for the repair work and when it went through council he suggested that Arnold be allowed to fix it within that budget.

Arnold and Violet Hodge worked very hard during Mr Hodge's mayoral year and Christmas time was no exception as they were expected to help serve the tea for the old folks.

Myra Pryor, Mayor 1995, and Russell Holden the parks superintendent planted a series of trees in Malpas Road as it was Mrs Pryor's intention to plant as many trees as possible during her term of office. Mr Holden is now the Town Clerk.

While Mr Hodge was on the city council there was a problem with the leats. In Truro we are accustomed to see water running through the channels alongside the pavement and a few years ago when parking in the town was much easier than it is today and visitors could park in the street, it was a regular sight to see the nearside passengers swing their legs out of the car and put their feet straight into the water. Occasionally a blockage will occur or some other problem will cause the leats to run dry in the town and inevitably this leads to complaints to councillors. When a property in River Street complained of water coming in their back door and running out of the front, the surveyor, Trevor Wilson, put dye in the water to prove that it was not water from the city's leat causing the problem. Unfortunately he found

The parks superintendent, Mr Foy, said that anything which had to be done should be done in the evenings when it would cause minimum disturbance in the town, so one evening they went up to the Waterfall Gardens and had a look at the weir. No water would flow so John Verran was told to pull up the manholes so that they could have a look, and they found that while their system had been shut down the county council had broken into their drains with their own drainage system. They rang the highways department but the county surveyor was unable to deal with them and they were advised to contact the district surveyor. He said they were the city's drains and he could do nothing about it but they persevered and asked how it happened that the county council's drains were in it. A camera put down there confirmed that they were correct and also that the spun concrete pipes had cracked. The thin tarmac in The Leats area of town behind Pydar Street was adequate when light traffic used the road on an occasional basis, but with the heavy delivery lorries that had been allowed to use that road regularly as access to the back of shops in Pydar Street, the weight had ruined the pipes. This explained the original complaint of flooding in the River Street property. They came to the conclusion that the water pipes needed to be lined with plastic ones and Arnold remembered seeing two pipes at St Day left behind after some repairs had been carried out there at least two years before. As co-operation between councils was common, a phone call was made to the Redruth council and Truro was given the plastic pipes.

With the old pipes lined they managed to get the water flowing as far as High Cross but it wouldn't go any further. In High Cross there was a square iron plate in the road which they were told to lift by Billy Trebell the works foreman. They lifted it and found a handle inside the hole. When they pulled the handle it lifted a square iron plate in the bottom of the hole and the water flowed on. This was a piece of old engineering dating from c.1700 as High Cross was subject to flooding and this would relieve the problem. So now the water flowed as far as Pearson's Ope but would go no further. At the Boscawen Street end of the opeway were another two square plates which had been there when the road was resurfaced with tarmac and were thus difficult to move. The water got as far as one but no farther and it was felt that the drain needed to be flushed out. As luck would have it Councillor John Christie, a retained fireman, was in Boscawen Street that very evening practising with the fire brigade and hosing down the Municipal Buildings. He was approached and asked if he could help and he saw no reason why not. The pump was brought over and the brass nozzle inserted into the drain, the pump was revved up and water forced down the drain. It worked, but in an instant Boscawen Street was awash with muddy water and had to be hosed down quickly before it caused an accident as cars were sliding all

The Mayor, Mrs Myra Pryor, takes a horse and carriage ride around Boscawen Street during Edwardian Week, 1995.

over the place. So far not one penny of the £500 set aside for the job had been touched but as Brian Cook offered to draw up a plan of the leats, which he later did (and they are still in use to this day), he was given a handsome decanter which cost £25, just half of the original amount suggested for the restoration of water in the streets.

Water of one sort or another has played a large part in the history of Truro and one of the civic duties performed at intervals is the beating of the river bounds. This is not done every year but when Dr Mabel Andrews was the Mayor the river bounds were to be beaten and the mayoral party set of in one boat with the band following behind in another. There was a bar on the Mayor's boat and unfortunately a couple of her male councillors made full use

of it on the journey to Messack Point. When the time came for the Mayor to transfer to the jolly boat to go ashore these two gentlemen decided to help her – although she was a very able lady and did not require any help from them. Nevertheless help she got, to the extent that as she transferred from one boat to the other her bottom dipped in the water. Not only did the mayoral robes get wet but so did that lady's knickers and she had to endure the rest of the day with cold, wet garments. Not surprisingly she preferred not to be helped in future, yet at the end of every council and committee meeting Alderman Arthur Behenna always managed to get to the coat stand before her and insisted on holding her coat for her to put on. It really made her cross but she could not be churlish and complain at such a simple courtesy!

When Lorrie Eathorne was the Mayor of Truro in 1987 her consort was Robert Mallett. On 16 October they went for the ride of a lifetime in a Nimrod. The trip took about six hours and during the period when Lorrie was sitting in the front with the pilot, Robert had to stand behind her and hold on to her seat. This was when the plane was doing manoeuvres and poor Robert became airsick but this soon disappeared when they were allowed to go back and sit down.

David Thomas of Truro City Council donned the armband worn by the town crier. It is a silver badge with a ship in full sail embossed on it representing the ship of Truro which is shown on the city coat of arms.

Chapter 11

✥

Schools & Education

Way back in 1547 Truro Grammar School was founded by Walter Borlase and over the years many pupils who were later to become famous passed through its doors. It is believed that the first schoolroom was in the porch of the old Parish Church but later a building in St Mary's Street became home to the school.

The school was no longer viable by 1877; although money had been spent on the building it was run down and the number of pupils had fallen so the school was re-formed. It became the Cathedral School and used the building now used by Social Services until 1960 then moved to Trewinnard Court before closing permanently. For the girls Truro High School for Girls was set up in 1897 after moving from Strangways Terrace where it had been a boarding establishment.

Sports day at the Cathedral School, c.1930, with the boys trying not to break any limbs on the obstacle course.

Another school in Truro is now known as Truro School, but began life as Truro College in 1880 and was first opened to pupils in 1881 (for boys only). Just as the Cathedral School was Anglican, the college was a Wesleyan establishment and its headmaster attended the Headmaster's Conference. Both these schools had grown out of a need for 'middle class' education as the system had been rather haphazard.

Over the years schools have come and gone and it is not possible to document them all here. Truro had elementary schools thanks to the churches. On the Church of England list there was St Mary's, St George's and St John's (infants), with another in Fairmantle Street that was used for a time as a training school for teachers who could then go off and teach in other parts of the county. In 1896 St Paul's School arrived and for many years the infants were at the bottom of Agar Road, the building being called Tregolls Manor these days and being used as a very smart residential home for the elderly. Meanwhile the juniors were at the top of Agar Road. For the Nonconformists there were schools known as British schools and there was one in City Road, then known as Back Lane, and one in Kenwyn Street as well as the day school near the Wesleyan St Mary's Chapel. Later, Bosvigo replaced these British schools.

Truro also had a Ragged School in Campfield Hill which was run by a Mr Edward Truncheon and this was for the poor and destitute to give them some sort of education. Secondary education was not the norm but for the better-off families there would also have been various academies and finishing schools.

There were dame schools in the town but mostly all trace of these has gone, although Mrs Clarice Mortensen Fowler knows that the upstairs of her house in Rosewin Row was used to house such an establishment. The boys were taught copperplate writing as most of them would end up working as clerks to lawyers where their handwriting would need to be elegant.

Schools were not answerable to the State but were privately run and it was the Education Act of 1870 that pulled things together. There had to be a place in school for every child and it would be compulsory for the children to attend so now not only did the elementary education need to be sorted out but also there had to be secondary education for all those who would not previously have received any. By 1902 it

Taken c.1946/47, this is an unusual photograph of students at work rather than a posed group. Left to right: Dinky Sweet, ? Sandercock, Giles Nixon, Bob Ragg and Mike Edwards. They are in the Art School which was the top floor of the Boys' Technical School in Union Place and they are modelling clay. Bob Ragg is seen making a pot in this photo but he was later known for making cockerels. Mike Edwards is making a pigeon.

Truro Cathedral School football team of 1930/31.

Here we see the smiling faces of children at St John's Church of England School in 1935. Left to right, back row: the teacher, Miss Ranale, ?, Mary Hill, George Vincent, John Keogh, Jean Waters, Betty Chapman; middle row: ?, Peter Evans, Frank Crewes, Audrey Chapman, Tony Rowe, Harold Barnicoat, Betty Sampson, ?; front: Douglas Endean, Gordon Whitford, Roy Vincent, Pauline Martin, ?, Ruth Cowling.

Here are the mistress and girls of St George's Church of England School, c.1920/21. Left to right, back row: Miss Rayworth, ?, ?, Dorothy Graa, ?, Gwennie Cookman, ?, Frances Annear, Winnie Elliott; middle row: Emily Burrows, ?, ?, ?, Phyllis Dingle, ? Anstis, Gladys Feltham, Florrie Ford; front: ?, Florrie Dennis, Evelyn Bird, Irene Trudgeon, May Waters, Irene Smith, Ada Scantlebury.

St Mary's Church of England School in 1922. There are only a few names to accompany this photograph unfortunately. Third from the left in the top row is Irene Holland and beside her are the Penrose twins. Percy Libby, Gordon Elliott, Enid Penhaligon and D. Holland are also in there somewhere!

St George's Church of England School had a football team who wore red and white striped shirts. This is the team of St George's AFC, 1924. Left to right, back row: ?, Bill Penhaligon, Captain Hallet, ?, ?, ? Richards; middle row: ?, ?, Graham Stone, Harold Kinsman, Charlie Holloway; front: Percy Martin ?, Harry Rapsey, ?, G. Bawden.

The tug-of-war teams battle it out at the Cathedral School sports day, c.1930. It must have been a very genteel occasion with the gentlemen in their Panama hats, the ladies in cloches (one with a Japanese sunshade) and the band to play between events.

A 1950s relay race.

Miss May Foreman was the headmistress of the County Grammar School for Girls from 1913–40.

was the county council who were responsible for schools and this meant that Bosvigo became an elementary school and Daniell Road took over from the Wesleyan day school in 1911. In 1906 the County Grammar School for Girls was formed and operated in Strangways Terrace before moving to its new premises in Treyew Road in 1925.

Sir Michael Sadler is seen at the opening ceremony of the new girls grammar school 15 December 1927.

Everyone has memories of their school days, some better than others! Although we all had to work and go through the trauma of exams, there had to be fun as well. At Truro School one day in the 1950s some of the boys of the third form decided that they would play a trick on the French master who was a native Frenchman and all the French text books were popped up into the attic. When he came in to start his lesson his first words were 'Now take out your text books.' All the desks were opened up and horrified cries of 'Mine has gone Sir, it's gone' filled the room. All the boys denied any knowledge and as far as we know the books are still in the attic to this day.

The same boys had a trick in store for another master who owned a bubble car that was his pride and joy. He used to park it in the lane in a passing place but one day the boys thought they would make it safer for him and manhandled it up some steps and deposited it beside the science block. At first the distraught master thought it had been stolen but then he saw it sitting in splendour in a place from which it was not possible to drive it away. Eventually he called a garage to remove it for him!

However, it was not all fun and games. In the early 1950s a pupil called Brian Vercoe died in an outbreak of polio and the school was closed for a few weeks. When it closed, the headmaster Mr Lowry Creed had a head of black hair, but when school returned only a few weeks later it is said that his hair was white.

On the speech day at Truro School it was the custom to invite the Mayor of Truro to attend and during the mayoralty of Arnold Hodge, 1969–70, after a council meeting just before speech day some of the older councillors asked if he could broach the subject of the hairstyle of some of the boys when he was at the school. The long hairstyles were completely alien to the old councillors and in those days some of the boys could even be seen eating in the street! At the school the Mayor was invited to coffee in the headmaster's house and as Mr Derek Burrell was an approachable man the Mayor brought the subject up. He expressed the grave concern of the councillors over the length of students' hair and the fact that they would eat chips in the street and explained that such things were

Before the new building in Treyew Road was opened at the end of 1927, the school was housed in Strangways Terrace. Here we see a gymnastics lesson in the garden there.

not done when the councillors themselves were younger! On their way to the speech day Mr Burrell told him that if they did not have a sixth form that was acceptable to the students, the parents would not send the boys to Truro School, in fact they had lost some pupils to other schools already and if there was no sixth form to finish the boys' education they would lose the whole school. Coming towards them were two long-haired students and Mr Burrell said that he could see the councillors' point but advised 'don't measure the depth of a boy's brain by the length of his hair but by his ability.' He looked at the boys approaching them and said, 'One of those boys will go to Oxford and the other to Cambridge.'

Going back even further, a brochure of Truro School c.1930 gives an insight into life for a boarder at the time. It states that:

The general health of the School is excellent due not only to the wonderfully healthy position of the School in the Cornish Riviera, but to the care and attention given to each boy individually. An experienced Nurse is in charge of the Dispensary and Sick Room, and minor health disorders are quickly remedied. Any case of infectious illness is immediately isolated.

Prospective pupils parents were also informed that:

Linen and cotton goods are sent to the steam laundry but all woollens are washed by hand in the School Laundry. All clean clothes are carefully aired before being given out to the boys.

On subjects of more interest to the boys the brochure states:

It is desirable that boys should not be too liberally supplied with pocket money. Arrangements can be made for a weekly sum to be given by the Headmaster and charged on the bill.

On the matter of boys wishing to supplement their diet it notes: 'A school tuck shop is organised by the masters, where boys may buy fruit, jam or good sweets. The entire profits are paid over to the Sports Fund.' One wonders what 'good sweets' were; perhaps local ones made by Furniss – who knows?

Many people will be sad to see this front view of the County Grammar School for Girls in the first stages of demolition. The foundation-stone was laid in October 1925 and it was in use as the grammar school until it became the sixth form college of Richard Lander School. It was demolished in 1993 to make way for Sainsburys supermarket.

Miss Mary Cobley was the head-mistress of the County School from 1947 until the grammar school closed.

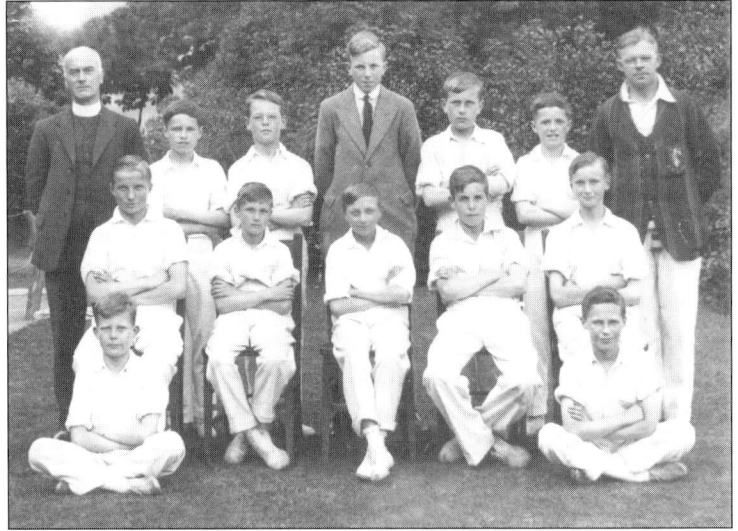

The Cathedral School cricket team, c.1931, with the headmaster Canon A.F. Welch back left and Mr F.H. Humpherson on the right. John Samuel Trounce is the fourth boy in the back row.

The Cathedral School had Army cadets and this photograph shows a presentation, c.1930. The lance corporal on the left gives us a clear picture of the uniform of the Duke of Cornwall's Light Infantry. The officer handing out the certificate appears to be a lieutenant-colonel.

The Truro School brochure, c.1930, reproduced this photograph by permission of The Times. It shows the gathering in 1927 when the Prince of Wales laid the foundation-stone for new school buildings. The new building was an assembly hall and school chapel.

Right: *Four boys appear to be doing some carpentry in the Truro School workshop, c.1930.*

Below: *The sports pavilion at Truro School was erected in 1920 in memory of the Old Boys who fell in the First World War.*

The hockey team of the grammar school, 1955/6. Mrs Passmore is the PE mistress and the names of the team are as follows, not necessarily in the order they are standing: A. Louis, R. Butson, A. Bertolucci, S. Opie, J. Simmons, C. Warren, A. Watts, Y. Prisk, J. Rule, R. Eva and C. Collins.

Bosvigo School, c.1959, and as so many children have done before and since, a class lines up in the playground for the annual photograph. Left to right, back row: Susan Grice, Sandra Franklin, Rebecca ?, Diana Buswell, ?, Claire Lidgey, ?, Susan Hewitt, Rosemary Stilliard, ?; third row: Doreen Cavill, Mary Cavill, Veronica Devlin, ?, ?, Lorna Kenward, Diane Thomas, ?, Valerie ?, Yvonne Metz; the second and front rows include: David Vinden, Roger Taylor, Frances Jenkins, Judith Thomas, James Beer, Geoffrey Jenkins, Brian McDowell, Peter Stethridge and Philip Mitchell (who is in the second row, second from right).

Chapter 12
✤
Events

Sometimes there will be an event that most people in the town remember in a very individual way depending on how closely they were affected by it. The demise of the Red Lion is one such event that has been discussed elsewhere in the book, but in the same era there were two other notable events that spurred the townsfolk into action. One was the building of Treliske Hospital and the offer to 'go and have a look'. The author and her father set off to have a tour of this wonderful new hospital one evening after he had come home from work and had his usual thorough wash with green Puritan soap. It was very effective for removing the soot and grime of the smithy and enabling him to get out of his working clothes and into something smarter. (These were the days when frilly decorated shower caps were all the rage; I had several given to me one Christmas but unfortunately the Cornish houses, many of them being little terraced cottages, were lucky to have an indoor bathroom, let alone a shower.) My homework done and school uniform abandoned for the day, we set out for the long uphill walk from Ferris Town to Treliske so that we could see the wonders of the hospital for ourselves and not feel out of things when we heard other people discussing it. I must admit that the memory is now all rather vague but I know we walked along gleaming corridors, in and out of wards and day rooms and visitors were even allowed into the theatres before they had been sterilised for use. There were lifts and a restaurant and the whole thing was a marvellous acquisition for Truro and Cornwall as a

The Queen and Mr Hawken Rowse, the Chairman of Cornwall County Council, at the new County Hall on her silver jubilee tour.

The gift to the Queen on the occasion of her silver jubilee was presented to her by the Chairman of Cornwall County Council.

The families of County Council employees were invited to be present in the grounds of the new County Hall to see the Queen in 1977 and many children took the opportunity to present her with flowers.

Geoff Carveth captured this gathering of the bards outside Truro cathedral in the 1980s. In September 2004 the Gorseth Kernow will be held in Truro and many bards will descend on the city and parade through the town to their ceremony on Lemon Quay and Back Quay (weather permitting).

whole. We were tired by the time we got home but that evening it seemed that all of Truro was having a look round the new hospital and it was great to be a part of it all.

The other event that got us all stirred up was the coming of Westward Television. We had all got used to our little black-and-white sets (ours bought from Edyvean and Lavanchy in River Street), but the one BBC channel was the only one we could get. Everyone was thrilled that ITV was coming and as well as the programmes we would have the adverts to watch. I am sure many people thought we were hard done by because down here in Cornwall we weren't advertised to as much as our friends and relatives up country. Not only that but if you had seen the advert before, you could pop out and put the kettle on or spend a penny.

The way that Westward advertised their coming was to send the 'Westward Train' down into the depths of Cornwall calling at the stations on the way and allowing the local people to go on board. So there we were, my father and I, on another evening setting off up the hill to the railway station where predictably we found most of Truro queuing to board the train. We wandered through the carriages looking at equipment and advertisements and meeting some of the stars of their programmes, news readers and presenters who of course meant nothing to us as yet. Again it is too long ago for me to remember clearly but the excitement was tangible and everyone seemed happy. We were all really looking forward to this opening up of our lives. Most of us came away with bright-blue badges with Westward and their logo of a white sailing ship emblazoned on them and those of us who were lucky (many had the bright idea of taking an autograph book along), came away with the autograph of the comedian and presenter Jack Train accompanied by his little drawing of a puffing train. We all trailed happily down the road back to the town clutching our little bags of loot, adverts, badges and autographs and waiting for the excitement that Westward would bring.

Actually it brought rather more excitement than anticipated to me and some of my school friends a few years later as we were selected to go on a quiz programme called 'Home Town'. Miss Cobley, the headmistress of the grammar school, had set the whole school a test of local knowledge, knowing that it was the results from the third year that she was particularly interested in as of course she knew that this programme was in the offing. She selected several girls (eight I think) to be interviewed by a Mr John Dobson from Westward who then selected a

team of four to represent Truro. The team – Avril Hiley, myself (Christine Mitchell), Judith Solomon and Corinne Waters – appeared on television three times before being knocked out in the semi final by the boys of Humphry Davy Grammar School, Penzance, who later won the trophy. Despite not going through to the end, the girls and two others who went as reserves had a very exciting time. Going to Plymouth on the train, being treated to a meal (usually egg and chips, nothing fancy!) at the Westward canteen at Derry's Cross and appearing on live television was quite a thing in 1963. One lady, whose name I forget, had been waiting to give her husband his tea but he was late home and arrived in the middle of the programme. She barely glanced at him and said, 'Come in, sit down and shut up, I'm watching our girls on the telly.'

Of course none of this would have been possible without electricity and as it happened Truro was rather a late starter in that respect. Gas was a different matter and by 1810 there was a gasworks on Lemon Quay. As it was one of the first in the country (and in the world), Truro was ahead of the game and many streets had gas lighting by the early 1820s. By the late 1870s many of the houses were lit by gas. Electricity, however, did not arrive until 1927 when Mrs Lodge switched on the power on 19 October, almost 40 years after it had first been suggested that the city have a supply.

A visit to Truro by any member of the royal family is always an event and the Queen's silver jubilee visit in 1977 gave most people a chance to see her. Thanks to John Allam and his ever-present camera we have a photograph of the gift given to the Queen and a photograph of her before he was asked to step back and stop putting his camera up the Queen's nose!

Every St Piran's Day, 5 March or the closest weekday, Truro plays host to the St Piran's Day Parade when as many Old Cornwall Societies as possible parade their banners through the city and other interested Cornish parties, including Mebyon Kernow, set off from St George's Church to walk to the cathedral where they gather in High Cross for a blessing then make their way to the tea and saffron buns while all the schoolchildren who have danced their way through the town are provided with biscuits and squash.

Another parade through Truro from Lander's Monument to the cathedral took place in 1997 when the 500th anniversary of the march from St Keverne to London passed through the city led by the banner of the Truro Old Cornwall Society behind the Mayor and civic party.

These days whenever Truro has a carnival it is organised by the Lions club and all the money raised goes to charity. Who organised the event in the past is not known but Truro has always had a good record for holding a carnival and this photo is thought to be from 1938/39. The drummer is holding a sign which advertised them as the 'Widdicombe Varmers & Wives Band' but only one name from the group is known. Top row left is Mr F. Lewis who was the landlord of the City Hotel.

Left: In 1994 some members of the Truro Old Cornwall Society who were going to the Royal Cornwall Show were enlisted to help with a surprise. Ian Stirling of the television feature 'Stirling Salute' was hoping to waylay Joy Stevenson as she enjoyed the show. As the showground at Wadebridge is rather large it was a problem to get her in the vicinity of the television stand at the right time. Just as she was needed it was discovered that she had popped to the ladies but as soon as she was in sight she was led to the stand and presented with a large bouquet of flowers by Ian Stirling as he had been told what a marvellous job she did in collating and storing as much of the old Cornish dialect as she could. Not only did Joy have a lovely surprise but as it was filmed she also appeared on the television that evening.

Left: *This Robert Roskrow photograph shows a brief but unusual time in Truro's history. The old police station had been demolished and the new station had been built but the rubble from the old one had yet to be removed.*

Another Roskrow photograph from 1974 shows Princess Anne at the official opening of the new police station. Staff inside the building were able to look out and see her as the building was actually erected the wrong way round, so all the corridors that were meant to be at the rear of the building out of sight are now a good vantage point to see what is going on in the world!

Whenever there is an event in Truro, like most other places in Cornwall it is accompanied by music. As far back as 1832 when the Reform Bill became law, after the gun had been fired and the flags hung out, there was a procession round the town with the band playing to help the celebrations. In June 1981 when the new Royal British Legion Club was opened in St Mary's Street the City of Truro Band under their conductor Rex Little led the parade of legion banners through Lower Lemon Street.

In the early 1980s Brenda Wooton, the folk singer (on the left) came to Truro to open the garden fête at Mountford House. She is seen here with the officer in charge of the home, Luella Carveth.

Rex Little waits with the fanfare parade of the City of Truro Band outside the Royal British Legion at the opening of the new club in 1981. The distinguished guests were to be greeted by a fanfare.

Lord Falmouth unveils the plaque in the British Legion club on Sunday 7 June 1981. Seen from the left are Ken Launder, Dick Jolley, Lord Falmouth, Maurice Trudgeon and the Mayor, Andrew Treseder.

It may not be unusual farther up country but in Cornwall snow is fairly rare which prompts people to record the event when it happens. Sister Gundry has stepped out of the old City Hospital to see for herself.

The summer of 2002 saw Truro visited by French Students. Geoff Carveth managed to capture this shot of them dancing round the band stand in Victoria Gardens while the Truro City Band played.

The professional international South African golfer Hugh Baiocchi came to Truro in the mid-1980s and gave a golfing demonstration at Truro Golf Club.

On the day of the Queen's Golden Jubilee many Truronians turned out to visit the area known as the Piazza between Back Quay and Lemon Quay and many of them wore red, white and blue. Many old friends bumped into each other and had time for a chat. Clarice Mortensen Fowler always enters into the spirit of any occasion and turned out in patriotic colours. Fred Mitchell, however, decided as it was a special day he would forsake the shorts he usually wears in summer for something more formal.

Today in local elections the turnout is usually very poor with barely 30 per cent of the electorate bothering to vote. On 26 January 1910 Boscawen Street was filled with Truronians eagerly awaiting the announcement of the result of the poll.

Truronians have always enjoyed their annual carnival but for several years it was not held due to insurance problems. When it was revived in 2002 it was as popular as ever and the parade was exceptional. This shows the float of the Truro Fairy King and Queen as they made their way into River Street.

In December 2003 fire fighter Lee Griffin hung over the Piazza for 44 hours. He had decided that he would like to raise money for the fire service's benevolent fund and was suspended with nothing more than water to sustain him. It was bitterly cold weather especially at night but he stuck to his plan and some of his colleagues were always on hand to rescue him if need be and to shake their buckets at the Christmas shoppers for donations. Mr Griffin's target was to raise £2,000 but he exceeded this amount.

Chapter 13

✦

Transport & How We Got There

In this view of Boscawen Street some time after 1922 the motorised taxis are lined up ready for hire down the middle of the road and a wonderful old lorry is preparing to drive up Lower Lemon Street.

Truro used to have trams many years ago but this does not seem to be a very well remembered fact and people do not seem to have any photographs of the vehicles in their albums. Janet Mitchell who looks after customers in Malletts coffee shop told the author that she used to have an old picture of one of her relatives dressed up and looking very smart with a beautiful hat. The thing which puzzled the family was that the hat appeared to have a number on top of it and they wondered whether the lady had entered for some sort of competition. Somehow the penny dropped and they realised that the photograph was taken back in the days when Truro had trams and she was simply standing in front of one of them, under the number!

In Truro during the 1950s most families were too poor to have transport of their own. Apart from the bicycle (and even that was not ideal for people who lived in a valley) most people turned to public transport to get out and about.

It was on Sunday afternoons during the summer that there was a mass exodus to the beach and often it was a quick look at the wind and weather that made the decision, Feock or Perran? Usually if it

looked as if the weather would be less than perfect on the north coast, then a trip to Feock was the answer. The Western National bus in its green livery blended in so well with the hedges that it might have disappeared altogether except for the fact that it was so big. The double decker left the depot just after lunch for the journey to Feock. Most youngsters scrambled for the upper deck as they could see so much more by being above the level of the hedge, but the adults, laden with picnics, rugs and cushions, tended to stay below. The bus stopped at the end of the route beside the telephone box and everyone piled out for the trek to Loe Beach. It was quite a step with all the gear to carry but at least it was mostly downhill on the way there. Coming back after an afternoon on the beach it was a steep uphill slog but by then the food had been eaten and the flasks were empty.

Truronians regarded Feock as their very own beach and tolerated the fact that it was no good to go there without cushions to sit on and plimsolls to wear into the water as it was so stony that it was a painful experience to walk the short distance from their own little patch of beach to the water. Those who had cars would arrive through the afternoon, not tied to the timetable of the bus like the others. Clifford Mitchell would arrive in his gleaming black Triumph Mayflower with his mother, Ethel, and amongst others Jack Lampier and his wife and family would arrive in their Standard Vanguard. One lady, Mrs Crago, who worked as a cook and housekeeper for the Webbers who owned the hardware shop at the bottom of Mitchell Hill, arrived at Loe Beach by boat as Mr Crago owned a little boat with an outboard motor that he used for fishing and taking his family out at the weekend. It was always a treat to be invited to travel home with them in the boat; avoiding the steep drag up to the bus was a definite plus and gliding upriver in the evening sun was a magical experience. Arriving at Malpas meant a slightly longer walk home but it was worth it for the experience of going upriver in the boat and anyway the flat walk up to the town past the park was a pleasant one.

Cornwall Motor Transport Company regularly held a dinner and dance for their employees and this photograph was taken in the Public Rooms, c.1927. The company had its own band and they are seated in the front and the fourth from the left is Jack Paddy with Johnny Harcourt fifth left. The managing directors are standing in a group behind on the right, keeping aloof from the rest of the crowd.

Alf Pryke stands beside a fire brigade Austin in the fire station under the viaduct. The car is not only equipped with a large spotlight but also a shiny bell.

In the early 1950s Jack Parnell worked as a store man as part of his job with the fire brigade and he often used his own BSA Golden Flash outfit to travel to St Agnes where the store was on the Cameron Estate, all of which has long since been demolished. Jack and his wife Betty also used the bike to have a 'holiday of a lifetime' when they went to London to stay with his brother George for a fortnight, a long way with a motor bike and sidecar.

Above: *A fire fighter gives his motor bike a polish at the fire station in St George's Road in the 1950s. It was his own bike and not one owned by the fire brigade so he was probably on a meal break or just posing with his pride and joy for the camera.*

Right: *Clarice Mortensen Fowler and the town crier, John Sweetman, are showing off a rather more modern motor bike c.2000. This photograph was not taken in Truro so John is not wearing the Truro uniform.*

One of the luxuries on offer at Loe Beach was that of frequenting the little tea shop across from the beach and perhaps buying a tray of tea to carry across the path and enjoy while sitting on your rugs and looking out at the view. The tea always tasted nicer, presumably because it had not been stewed in a flask, and when it was gone, the children would carefully carry the tray back for their parents and be allowed to buy an ice-cream.

Perranporth was different as it was so much more spread out. Once you stepped off the bus you might not see your travelling companions any more until the return trip as everyone disappeared off in different directions, usually to meet up with other members of the family who would be in their regular place on the beach. Arriving at the usual family spot in the sandhills you would be made welcome, told where the cousins were playing, invited to share anything they had and it would turn into an extended family picnic. By the time the bus rumbled back to Truro again it was early evening and thoughts would turn to school on Monday.

The traffic was so light in the 1950s and early '60s that small groups of girls walking home from the grammar school (particularly at lunch time) would give themselves a number and take turns at 'owning' any vehicle that came up Richmond Hill and Station Road. The first girl might get a nice little car, the second a tractor which would send them all off into fits of laughter and it was not unusual for the third and fourth girl not to 'own' anything at all by the time they had reached the bottom of the hill.

Sunday school and church outings, certainly at St Paul's Church, usually meant the hire of a coach which was a bit more up-market than the bus. One such outing was a trip to the beach at Swanpool which was blessed with lovely weather until a few minutes before the coach was due to collect everyone and a

This photograph of Boscawen Street c.1915 shows various modes of transport. There are horse-drawn vehicles, an open motor car, a bicycle and at the end of the street in front of the bank is the hut which has appeared all over the town at different times and was a shelter for the taxi drivers and ended its days as the car park attendant's hut on The Green. We know that this picture was taken after November 1914 as the clock has a white face. The original clock with a black face was lost in a fire when the whole clock tower collapsed into the council chamber beneath.

We are looking down Lower Lemon Street towards the Red Lion in the early 1950s with only two vehicles to be seen. The lorry is an O-type Bedford which was an immediate postwar vehicle and the pick-up is a 1951 Austin A55.

downpour soaked them. Another church outing was to St Ives and on that occasion the train was used. Perhaps it just depended whether the selected venue had a railway station or not. Mrs Phyllis Williams, a stalwart churchgoer at St Paul's, was used to something even better than the run-of-the-mill coaches. She had a sister who lived in Worcester and she used to go up to see her sometimes and travel on the Royal Blue. This was the height of luxury and she used to book her seat too! Even if she didn't travel on it herself for a while it was often in our thoughts as her sister used to buy baskets of Victoria plums in season and send them down on the coach. When this happened Phyllis would meet the coach and she and

her neighbour Margaret Mitchell would have a jam- and tart-making session. For weeks in advance the jam pots would have been washed and stored instead of being thrown away and soon the cupboards would be well filled with preserves.

There were many country buses which served the rural areas and which lumbered into the city bulging with passengers. Miss Liz Hotten, a member of Truro Old Cornwall Society who was brought up at Ladock, said that the Ladock bus was usually over-loaded, especially on market day (Wednesday) and by common agreement all those who were standing in the aisle would crouch just before the bus got to the police station at the end of Tregolls Road so that it looked as if the bus carried just seated passengers. Once they were safely past the police station every-one would get up again. Usually it would be the Lidgey bus that would cover Tregony and the Roseland, and Bennetto's was the bus used to get to us to see the grandparents at St Columb Major. It never got closer than St Columb Road then went off towards Newquay so the Grandpa had to get the old Hillman out and fetch us.

Going back farther to the 1900s many people liked to travel by boat and a day out often involved board-ing one of the pleasure steamers at Worth's Quay and steaming off to Falmouth. One of the steamers was the *Princess Victoria* which started work on the river c.1907 and happily plied her way between Truro, Falmouth and St Mawes for many years, together with the *Queen of the Fal* and the *New Resolute*. The *Princess Victoria* was taken over by the Admiralty in 1941 and never came back to Truro again; she would have been elderly by the end of the war anyway. We have an account of a Sunday school outing on the river which gives us an insight into a 'treat' on the river in days gone by:

In February 1974 Truro was flooded and some drivers were caught unawares!

Above: *The bus station was not a very elegant building but we all got used to seeing it there. This picture was taken in 1999 shortly before it was taken down to make way for new shops on Lemon Quay.*

Left: *Harold and Audrey Whitburn gave their nephew Brian Pascoe a job cleaning up their yard c.1939. Their United Yeasts van is parked behind him in their premises in New Bridge Street.*

Robert Roskrow took this photo in 1977 when a meat lorry overturned outside the old County Hall and the oncoming Vauxhall had to steer carefully around it. For any police officer having to deal with the event, the number plate of the lorry must have caused some amusement, RTA being a road traffic accident to a policeman.

Worth's Quay was not only the embarkation point for river trips but also a pleasant place to have a picnic or just sit admiring the view and the water (providing the tide was in!). The pretty pavilion was built in 1911.

Three young men squat on the grass for a photo on Worth's Quay, c.1952. From the left they are Louis Roberts, Harold Barnicoat and Stan Thomas. Behind them and to the left beyond the end of the old Boscawen Bridge are the Palace Buildings and the Britannia Inn.

Memories of the River Fal & Truro
by Jack Parnell (1911–80)

My first memory goes back to a period not long after the Great War of 1914–18, to my Sunday School days in fact. In those days particularly for those children with a full attendance card, we had what was known as the Annual Tea Treat. This was usually held in the form of a trip down the Fal to St. Mawes. Not always of course; sometimes it turned out to be a char-a-banc trip to Carbis Bay or Falmouth, or possibly Perranporth. All this was very nice and most kids agreed that it could be a good day out, as long as it was fine weather. Unfortunately however, the great day was not always, not very often in fact, as fine as one would hope. This business of folks talking about how wonderful the summers used to be as compared with today, is a matter of distance lending enchantment, one is inclined only to remember the odd long beautiful summer day. There were periods when we enjoyed many days of sunshine and warmth; there still are, but these spells don't always come at the right time to suit everyone. Consequently we only remember the particular days when we were fortunate enough to be able to go out and enjoy it. The fact that somebody else had his holiday during a wet period did not bother us at all!

I remember school treats which provided all sorts of conditions. I particularly remember one that offered 'the lot' in the way of weather conditions. The morning was extremely promising; the sun shone down on all the parents and children who gathered, more or less happily, at Worth's Quay awaiting the great moment when we were to embark on either the Queen of the Fal or her sister ship the Princess Victoria. They were steam ships specially designed for river work. They did not draw much water, being flat-bottomed, but there was plenty of room on deck, two decks in fact. There was the main deck or one could go upstairs to sit on wide wooden seats curved roughly to the shape of one's back when in a sitting position but I don't think anyone was ever very comfortable on them. I know the women keeping a weather eye on their own particular children (who were milling about the crowded deck) were not in any way comfortable. They would sit on the very edge of the seat, bolt upright, some having lost sight of their excited progeny immediately on embarking, others clinging tightly on to the reluctant hands of mischievous offspring who appeared hell bent on taking over the ship. It would not be until the ship's steam hooter hissed and roared its signal that it was about to depart, that the other kids rushed back to the arms of their mothers. The sudden and alarming noise of the hooter was frightening I must admit. For a second one could look round at a hundred frightened faces, frozen into immobility. Some would then rush to find their mothers if they could remember where they'd put them! It would soon be over and the ship's company would quickly settle down to watch the warehouses glide past. Then Harvey's Timber Yard would loom ahead and some of the men working there would pause a moment to wave back to the shouting children as we passed. Some of our company would have fathers working there, no doubt fathers who would be thanking the Good Lord that they had to be working on that day of the 'Treat'. In fact, now I come to think of it, not many dads were to be found among us, it was always mum's job! The only men to be seen were the people we knew from Sunday School, perhaps with the odd superintendent of the area, or district, or whatever.

By now, approaching Sunny Corner, some of the more voracious of the youngsters began to dig into their mothers' handbags looking for food, or perhaps they had been too excited to eat breakfast that morning, so, bags for buns, sandwiches and the like, so we were fairly well off. Fortunately both my brother and I were good sailors, in that we were not affected by the rough conditions. Mind, I did not feel too happy when a child sitting opposite me on a seat just inboard of the gunwale of the ship turned about suddenly and with a wail of despair, threw his entire breakfast overboard! More details of these personal disasters I won't go into here and now, you probably get the picture! It was happening all over the ship.

At Turnaware, where the river opens out to its widest to enter the Carrick Roads, the prospect was by no means pleasant. A south east wind carrying rain in plenty blew into the sharp bows of The Queen. Still, Cap'n Benney (I think it was him) was hired to take this mass of now apprehensive humanity to St. Mawes so that they might enjoy a day out on the river! So now, whether they liked it or not, this he proceeded to do! The old ship threw up her head and with thick dark smoke flattening out of her funnel and half choking those unfortunates sitting in the stern seats, ploughed her way proudly on. She pitched into the rollers (still powerful even though they had left the open sea some six miles behind them) and rolled each time her bows came up for air.

Panic ensued, screaming children and in many cases, screaming mothers, rolled about in their seats pleading with a crew member passing towards the engine room, to turn round and go back before we were all drowned. However he did not seem unduly perturbed and grinning a little self-consciously, passed on his way. I believe it was his attitude of unconcern, coupled with the soft assurances of the Sunday School teachers, which eventually quietened them down a little, white faced and clinging desperately to any hand hold, they faced the rest of the journey to St. Mawes, not with equanimity exactly but with a desperate calm determination to see it through for the sake of the children, all of whom, if truth be told, would have given their tea-treat bun to be home out of it!

Of course we were not in any real danger; these old boats could face up to all the weather the river could throw at them but these folk were not sailors, except on this once a year trip, so one could not expect them to accept this horrible discomfort without some kind of protest. Still, the following year, the same crowd turned up ready to have another try and still hoping for that elusive sunny day.

After a long half hour during which the old ship groaned and protested her way along the Carrick Roads and into the comparative shelter of the St. Mawes entrance, her bedraggled passengers huddled together, very unhappy but thankful that this, to them a nightmare trip, was nearly over as she was manoeuvred

Taken in the 1960s, this is a view of Enys Quay with the premises of C.W. Brown, decorator and sign writer, a cabinet maker and picture framer, and Banfield Cars. The cars include a Standard Vanguard facing us with a Heinkel Messerschmitt beside it. The Morris 1000 is between two stylish touring cars. The quay was built by Samuel Enys to export his tin and copper in the early part of the eighteenth century.

stuffing their faces and running happily about, the children were the last to notice that the sun no longer shone upon them so brightly, nor that the wind was not just that which was created by the movement of the ship. It became colder too. Gradually it became evident that this day, which had started with such promise, was hinting at menace.

The rain began as we were approaching the King Harry area, the main deck became more crowded as those who had chosen the top deck to be in the sun, descended upon us. We did not mind though, huddled together we were a little warmer. My mother had chosen a spot underneath the upper deck where we were reasonably dry and warm – the engine room was only just below the other side of the bulkhead against which we leaned. It was not crowded there because the warm oily smell emanating from the engine room did not seem to agree with most of our companions, more especially perhaps those who had chosen to raid their mothers'

King Harry Ferry as it was c.1907 when this card was posted. It was sent from St Mawes to someone in Falmouth and says that he is 'having a fine time carrying hay'. There has been a ferry crossing there for many years, some people believing that it got its name from Henry VIII as he is supposed to have travelled across the ferry on his honeymoon with Anne Boleyn. It is more likely, however, that the Harry in question was Henry VI as Tolverne Chapel had been dedicated to 'Our Lady and King Henry' by the Arundell family of Tolverne. The King Harry Steam Ferry Company was founded in 1888 with their first crossing being made in September 1889. As the first ferry ran until it was replaced in 1913 this must be a picture of the first one.

The name of Hicks was well known in Truro to the motoring fraternity. Hicks Garage has been spotted in old photos of the city in many different locations over the years. They were in River Street and Kenwyn Street in the 1900s, in recent memory they were beside Boscawen Bridge then on Lemon Quay. In the mid-1960s Hicks had a very modern showroom with a circular window in City Road where in 1966 a Jaguar motor car was displayed and, on another occasion, the brand-new mini drew everyone's attention. This picture was taken c.1900 and shows Samuel James Hicks (born 22 April 1872) and his bride Ada Butson.

alongside the harbour wall. Now that the Sunday School contingent realised that they were safe, they were curiously reluctant to leave the ship and venture up the quay into the rain and wind.

They found however that their plight had not gone unnoticed. Officials of the local chapel were there waiting to greet them and they soon had a crocodile leading away to the Sunday School where tea would be served to the assembled company and later, out would come the famous ' tea-treat' buns. These were large round saffron affairs, one of which would cover the average dinner plate. Why we all looked forward so much to this vast amount of stodge I cannot say, but it was a fact and probably still is, although in these days of inflation I don't suppose such monstrosities would even be on offer. Very few of us could ever chew our way through to the end of one but would creep sheepishly along to mum and ask her to put the other half in her handbag to be eaten later. It very seldom was; on the return trip, if the weather conditions were the same as on the outward trip, nobody wanted any food for they were too busy getting rid of the first half of the bun.

On this particular day, as the wind whistled round the old building, the teachers and one or two of the more courageous mothers, organised games and competitions, and being children of nine and under, we soon forgot our terrors of a short time ago and joined in with gusto. There were prizes to be won, packets of sticky sweets, ice creams and the like, everything in fact guaranteed to put the small tummy in dire jeopardy as later the steamer put her nose down to meet the first wave outside the harbour. However, that came later on. Right now we were enjoying our brief freedom.

About 4.30pm the festivities ground to a halt with most of us practically exhausted by our efforts. It was then we heard the mournful cry of the hooter as it floated

towards us, well, not exactly floated as much as hurled by the fierce wind which still held sway outside. This of course came from The Queen *or the* Princess *calling all happy passengers to come aboard for the return trip. Once more the reluctant crocodile formed and wended its way down through the steep streets of the old town, looking more like a column of early Christian martyrs going to meet their doom! Arriving back at the harbour we were glad to notice, those of us with any interest left in the proceedings, that the rain had almost stopped although the wind still blew strongly from the south east. Fortunately the Captain relented, or perhaps he had had enough also, for he did not provide us with the extra special treat of a trip round the Black Rock on the way home. That, I think, would have been the absolute end for most of us. It had been a little less than half tide and ebbing when we had left Truro that morning. Now as we turned round beneath St. Mawes castle, we had both wind and tide with us. The old ship picked up her skirts and ran up to Turnaware in fine style, a few kids left their tea-treat buns behind for the delectation of the kind of fish who would eat that sort of thing. On the whole spirits perked up as we left beautiful Trelissick on our left or should I say port side, this being something of a nautical tale, and entered the narrower and sheltered reaches of the river.*

Soon we were waving to everyone ashore at Tolvern, then Malpas and by the time we had wended our way through the tricky channel of the Truro River and were approaching the home port, we, that is the children, had almost forgotten earlier terrors and generally concluded that in spite of the weather we had all had a jolly good time. Such is the resilience of children. As for the mothers? Well, I think it took them a little longer before they began to look forward to the next Sunday School Annual 'Treat'!!

A good time was had by all!

Chapter 14

The Changing Railway Scene

by Eric Irons

Rather surprisingly, the first railway to reach Truro was not from the Devonshire end of the county but rather from the far west. The West Cornwall Railway, itself an expansion of the earlier Hayle Railway, reached Truro in 1852 and was officially opened on 25 August with the main celebration taking place at Penzance from where the greatest enthusiasm for the formation of the line had emanated.

The original station was situated at Highertown just short of the point from which the current Falmouth line diverges from the main line, the site now being overseen by the County Arms public house. This, however, was a short-lived facility as it was supplanted three years later when the line was realigned so that it continued to follow the northern side of the Calenick stream. After a short cutting, the line turned sharp north to run alongside the Truro river and terminate at Newham. The station here was a more imposing structure and was within easy walking distance of the then town centre, thus avoiding the steep climb (via Chapel Hill) to Highertown. The station at Newham was of wooden construction with an overall roof spanning two tracks, and although it too lost its passenger service very quickly it remained in situ even after the goods yard closed in 1972. Regrettably this historic structure was subsequently quietly demolished to make way for the modern development of Newham.

However, before the demise of the railway at Newham it gained an, albeit too brief, new lease of life following the completion in 1957 of a new modern coal-fired gas power station. Whereas coal for the former gasworks situated at Lemon Quay came by way of boat, the new power station was rail served; the works being situated on the site currently occupied by the Royal Mail sorting office. This increase in traffic sometimes resulted in two trains per day making the trip to Newham. Sadly the advent of North Sea Gas and its associated pipeline system brought about the closure of the works in 1969 with consequent loss of traffic to the railway.

The West Cornwall Railway was of course a relatively small undertaking even by the standards of the 1850s as by this time railway mania had gripped the country. As early as 1843 ideas were being floated to link Cornwall with the ever expanding rail network in the rest of the country. Brunel's Great Western from London to Bristol had opened in 1841 and by 1844 the Bristol and Exeter Railway was welcomed in Exeter. It was not, however, until 1849 that the long-suffering South Devon Railway, with its ill-fated experiment with atmospheric propulsion, reached Plymouth.

Although the West Cornwall Railway was the first into Truro work had nonetheless already started on the construction of a line from Truro to Plymouth. However, financial constraints prevented any real progress being made when the Truro to St Austell section got going again. This was to be the Cornwall Railway to run from Plymouth to Falmouth and whose proposed route was to be the forerunner of today's main line. At about the same time a start was made westwards from the site of the proposed Cornwall Railway Station resulting in the construction of the present-day cutting and tunnel at Highertown.

By 1859 the line from Truro to Plymouth was completed following the opening of the Royal Albert Bridge at Saltash. The new Cornwall Railway station, being on the site of the current railway station, was opened on 4 May. In anticipation the West Cornwall Railway had already re-laid track from its former Highertown station site through Highertown tunnel and on into the new Cornwall Railway station. Within a week of the opening of the new station virtually all West Cornwall Railway trains were re-routed into the new station. This sealed the fate of Newham as a passenger station which closed entirely to passengers on 16 September 1863. However, as previously mentioned, goods facilities continued to survive until as late as 1972.

Money problems continued to plague the Cornwall Railway and it was not until 24 August 1863 that the remaining section of the line to

The steam engine 'The City of Truro' was the first one to reach the speed of 100 miles per hour and is beautifully preserved. For several years during the 1990s the Chamber of Commerce organised themed 'Edwardian Weeks' and during one of them the engine was brought to Truro and placed in High Cross. Paddy Bradley of Redruth took this photograph during a brief spell when it was not covered by sightseers.

A view of the Waterfall Gardens, c.1900, gives a clear picture of the wooden viaduct of Isambard Kingdom Brunel spanning the valley.

Falmouth was finally opened. The Cornwall Railway had adopted Brunel's broad gauge seven feet and one quarter inch for all its lines whereas the West Cornwall Railway, albeit more on grounds of economy rather than farsightedness, had laid its tracks to Stephenson's preferred gauge of four feet eight and a half inches. Although referred to in the early-nineteenth century as narrow gauge, this was destined to become the standard gauge of most of the world's railways. However, in 1864 the Cornwall Railway gave notice, as it was entitled to do under the terms of the West Cornwall Railways Enabling Act, that it required the West Cornwall to lay a broad-gauge track. This the West Cornwall achieved by simply laying an additional line alongside its own track. This resulted in mixed-gauge track between Truro and Penzance. The avoidance of having to change trains at Truro was of considerable benefit to both passengers and goods customers.

Where the lines (respectively) to Penzance and Falmouth parted company, just west of Highertown tunnel, two little curiosities evolved in the railway scene. The first was that the junction was bestowed with the name of Penwithers – albeit that nowhere was there any landmark with this spelling, there being 'Penwethers' or even 'Penweathers' but none with an 'i'. However, this spelling was subsequently adopted by the Great Western Railway and British Railways and so it is that this spelling now features in all railway literature and on Ordnance Survey maps.

The second aberration concerns the evident intention to construct a line directly linking the West Cornwall's Newham line to that of its route into the new station thus enabling trains to operate between the two stations without the need for reversal. However, although the earthworks were clearly completed, there is no record of any track ever having been laid. The cutting which resulted from the excavation remained in railway ownership well into the last century and within this depression a pond was formed. This pond, surrounded by low trees and bushes, became the haunt of many children over the years, providing an abundance of tadpoles, newts and frogs. The pond was unusual in that while it had no determinate inlet or outlet, it never became noticeably stagnant. Known by a number of names, it was best remembered by children in the area as Turkey Pond.

The low embankment formed in the 'v' of this uncompleted junction was a good vantage point from which to view the trains at close quarters and in later years it became the focus of many a trainspotter. Sadly both of these pastimes are no longer of any attraction and although parts are accessible to the public, much is largely overgrown and impenetrable with sometimes little or no water in the pond.

Because of the expense of laying an additional line to accommodate broad-gauge trains, control of the West Cornwall Railway passed to its associated bankers consisting of the Great Western, Bristol and Exeter and South Devon railways. Ten years later following the amalgamation of the 'associated companies' into the Great Western Railway control of the Cornwall Railway was also gained by the GWR although it was not until 1889 that the GWR gained full ownership.

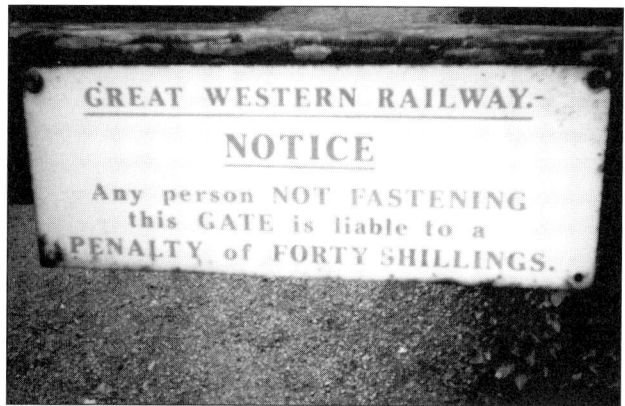

An old enamel sign from the days of the Great Western Railway still survives in a village near Truro. The railway line no longer goes anywhere near the gate and a 40-shilling fine would be difficult to find but it is nice to see the old sign still there.

The Cornwall Railway station, although much larger than that of Newham, also had the advantage of an overall roof and, so it would appear from the Cornwall census of 1891, refreshment facilities, as the census records under the heading of railway employees, that three ladies were employed at the time as 'refreshment room assistants'! The census also reveals that one John King of Campfield Lodge was employed as a 'viaduct watchman'. Such very long timber viaducts would no doubt have been vulnerable to flying sparks from the locomotives.

While at first the station received much acclaim, complaints that it was draughty and dirty began to be voiced towards the end of the nineteenth century. It therefore fell to the GWR to put matters right and this it did by constructing a brand-new station of considerably larger proportions and which with subsequent minor improvements and extensions remains, over 100 years later, as Truro's station of today.

The rebuilding of Truro station began after the conversion of the broad gauge to standard gauge in 1892. By this time the line to Penzance had become

A steam train crosses Brunel's old wooden viaduct at Penweathers, c.1900 or possibly earlier.

the main line rather than Falmouth and because it was of mixed gauge the conversion became centred at the ends of the last remaining section of solely broad-gauge main line to be converted, namely between Exeter and Truro. This massive undertaking was to be completed in two days, between 20 and 21 May 1892 and was also to include the Falmouth branch which was an exclusively broad-gauge line.

Truro's new station was opened in 1900 and was complemented by the opening of a new locomotive depot, goods yard and marshalling sidings. Adjacent to the engine shed was a workshop for the repair of rolling stock. Extensive earthworks were required for the construction of these new facilities.

The final major progression of the railway scene in Truro took place in 1904 with the construction of the two substantial double-track masonry viaducts to replace Brunel's hitherto single-line viaducts. Were it not for the intrusion of high ground now occupied by the law courts Truro would have been straddled by a bridge nearly one mile long. As it is the longer eastern viaduct is 437 yards long, making it the longest viaduct in Cornwall. This is Truro viaduct

but locally often referred to as Moresk viaduct and is undoubtedly the second most striking landmark in Truro. In his book on Cornwall John Betjeman describes it as 'the finest building added to Truro since the cathedral.' Except for the intrusion of the court building, the viaducts provide the most magnificent view of a cathedral and its city anywhere in Britain, exceeding even that of Durham.

The viaduct nearest the station is Carvedras viaduct but sometimes locally known as St George's. This latter title is of course derived from the name of the church beneath it. Interestingly the church in return has an unusual feature connecting it with the railway. On the wall of the sanctuary behind the high altar is a large mural in the form of a montage. The left side depicts various Truro landmarks of around about the 1920s with Carvedras viaduct most prominent and complete with a Great Western train. On the right side are various notable features from the African continent. The theme is one of the glorification of heaven and earth. The painting is accommodated on 13 separate boards which were formed to correspond with the shape of the building and entailed the blocking up of the windows in the apse. The artist was Miss Stephany Cooper, the daughter of a former chancellor of Truro cathedral.

With the completion of the new viaducts the Cornish main line was then double track throughout from St Germans to Penwithers junction. This was a time of prominence for Truro. With its new station, locomotive depot and other facilities, it became one of the major centres of the railway in Cornwall. The year 1903 saw the opening of the branch line from Chacewater to Perranporth followed by an extension to Newquay two years later with some services running through to Truro. Thus the importance of Truro as a pivotal centre for transport was further increased.

Truro had already been chosen as the site for the cathedral of the reconstituted Cornish bishopric and in consequence was granted the style of city by Royal Charter. The pre-eminence of Truro over rival Bodmin for county status was further compounded at this time by the restructuring of local government with the consequent formation of county councils. Truro was selected for the headquarters of Cornwall County Council and County Hall was built almost alongside the newly constructed station. This inevitably resulted in a considerable increase in commuter traffic, thus further enhancing the number of passengers using Truro station.

On the freight side Truro now had two goods depots, that at Newham and one to the immediate east of the station at the top of Richmond Hill. In addition and again coming into being at the turn of the nineteenth century, a siding was constructed on the high ground between the two viaducts. This was to serve the cattle market which was then based at the top of Edward Street on the site now occupied by the Courts. Market day was Wednesday and, ostensibly, for the benefit of market users certain public houses were permitted to remain open all day. One such establishment was the refreshment rooms at Truro station.

Of the station itself, this was built on a large scale and had the look of importance. It was probably more prepossessing than any other station in Cornwall, save possibly for Penzance. The main offices and facilities were, unusually for buildings in Cornwall, constructed of small red brick. Architecturally the style is said to be French and in which case it will have something in common with the cathedral. There is no similar design of station in Cornwall; the nearest likeness being that of Torquay but not in red brick. The main station buildings were on the down side, fronting on to Coronation Terrace and what by then had become Station Road. Platform one was the main down platform with a bay

Frederick Trebell on the left is presumably with his fellow workers of gang 17 just outside Truro. No fancy uniforms or protective gear for them; flat caps and picks seem to have been the order of the day!

for Falmouth line departures at its western end. The large island platform was host to platforms two and three, both being through-line platforms. In the 1950s British Railways dispensed with the term bay which then became one with the others being respectively renumbered two, three and four. The island platform was connected to the main down-side platform by two covered footbridges. The fact that they were covered immediately denotes the importance of any station but to have two is rare on any part of Britain's railway system. In the West Country Exeter Central had two footbridges but one of these was isolated from the main station buildings.

With the appointment of G.J. Churchward as Chief Mechanical Engineer to the GWR in 1902, more powerful locomotives were introduced resulting in much longer trains. It was not long therefore before the platforms at Truro were extended. This lengthening took place on the western side and resulted in the platforms being taken under the footbridge connecting Station Road with Bosvigo Lane. Known for much of its lifetime as Black Bridge this provided a fine vantage point from which to view the movement of trains in the station along with the shunting operations that took place on almost a 24-hour basis every day except Sundays. It also resulted in the main down platform having two water cranes as the one that was originally installed when the platform was shorter was never removed and indeed remained in use until the end of steam working – yet another distinctive feature of the Truro railway scene.

Almost without exception with every through working of a passenger train, the locomotive would take on water at Truro. There was a water crane at the locomotive end of each platform with one at both ends on platform three which was signalled for either way working. These cranes would pour hundreds of gallons of water into the tenders or tanks of a locomotive in a matter of two to three minutes. Special arrangements therefore had to be available. To facilitate this a large water tower was erected at the eastern end of the main down platform. The water for this did not come from the mains but directly from the River Kenwyn running beneath Carvedras viaduct. The water was drawn directly from the river and pumped up to the top of the viaduct from where it was piped to the water tower. The pumping station was housed in a sheet metal building at the bottom of the playing field. Although the building is no longer there, the pipe remains in place duly attached to a pier of the viaduct at the bottom of Hendra Road.

Black Bridge provided a marvellous grandstand from which to view the work of firemen as they prepared the locomotive of west-bound trains for the stiff climb ahead. After taking on water the fireman would bring the coal forward in the tender and begin shovelling fuel into the firebox of the engine. The longer trains would pull up to the outer water crane and this gave spectators on the bridge a bird's-eye view of operations on the footplate. The immediate climb out of Truro to Highertown tunnel was at 1 in 60 and from a standing start with a heavily loaded train, this was no easy task even for the most skilled driver. Many an unassisted locomotive would 'lose its feet' and provide a fine spectacle as its driving wheels slipped on the greasy rails as its driver strove to gain adhesion. Sometimes a train would move slowly forwards only to stop again. This was because the rear coaches of the longest trains would extend beyond the end of the platform. The knowing observer would also be aware that such activity invariably heralded the provision of a banking locomotive. This was an engine provided to assist the train out of the station by pushing from the rear. This was a highly spectacular performance with both train engine and banker working vigorously. Although this was a very routine practice, regrettably there is very little photographic record of this activity.

Another operation that could be advantageously viewed from the Black Bridge was the arrival of the circus train. Unlike today's compact road-bound and animal-less affairs, the circuses between the wars and indeed right up until the 1950s were on a much larger scale. These were the circuses of Chipperfield, Bertram Mills and Billy Smart. Just beyond the Black Bridge of the line leading into the bay platform is a loading bank from which a ramp leads up to Station Road. From here the circus animals that were fortunate enough not to be cage bound were unloaded and walked to the showground in Treyew Road. The parade of the animals was much anticipated not only by the children of the city but also by gardeners and allotment holders who would be ready with bucket and shovel, with the elephant dung much prized!

Between watching the many activities of railway working that could be witnessed from Black Bridge a quick dash down the steps to Bosvigo Lane would bring one to James Martin's orchard. Almost every variety of apple seemed to be there. One now long forgotten was the magnificent American Mother. This was the stuff of fairy tales but it did not belie its deep-red colour and massive size, being sweet and juicy. The orchard is now long gone, having been supplanted by Bosvean Gardens.

From the turn of the nineteenth century Truro continued to flourish as a railway centre. The First World War inflicted a great toll on the working of

Looking down the slope which was used for the animals from the circus to leave the train towards the shed where once a turntable was used to turn the engines.

A parade of circus animals c.1900 makes its way along Back Quay outside the premises of N. Gill and Son.

Britain's railway system. During this period the operation of the railways was taken over by the Government. At this time there were 168 separate railway companies of which by far the largest in terms of route mileage was the Great Western. Such was the success of the Railway Executive in co-ordinating the running of the railways it was widely believed that nationalisation would follow. Instead the Railway Act of 1921 brought about the grouping of all but a few of the railways into four new ones based largely on geographical boundaries. Of the larger of the railway companies only the Great Western was to retain its name, and so continuity of railway ownership at Truro continued from 1889 until the end of 1947.

The intervening period between the wars saw very little change in either the structure or operation of the railways in and around Truro. There was, however, one important social development. Railways are a very labour-intensive industry and involve a great deal of shift working. To aid communication with its workforce and for the better welfare of its workers generally the GWR encouraged its employees to live as near to each other as possible. In aid of this and where there were large centres of railway employment it embarked on a system of building low-cost quality housing for its employees. Truro was one such centre and between 1925 and 1927 36 semi-detached houses were built between Daniell Road and Green Lane. These are the houses at Green Close. At first they were largely occupied by the engine-driving staff who because of their better pay were best able to afford the rent. The locomotive men were also very union orientated and seemed able to negotiate better terms and conditions of work than perhaps other less essential grades. Consequently for many years this estate became known as 'Little Moscow'! In due course and following the management of the estate passing to the Devon and Cornwall Housing Association all occupiers were given the opportunity of purchasing their homes. This was unanimously agreed and now all the properties are privately owned with only one retired railwayman and two widows of railway employees in residence. There is nothing now to associate the estate with the GWR save that one property has been given the name 'The Railway House'. For those who are not aware of the history of the estate this will no doubt give rise to much puzzlement in years to come as the area is not situated noticeably close to any railway installation.

In 1941 Truro became the first station in Cornwall to be equipped with a loud-speaker system. With its refreshment rooms and book stall this further enhanced the atmosphere of Truro as an important main-line station.

The public-address system was no doubt very useful during the years of the Second World War when many special troop trains ran up and down the country.

The single most violent act of wartime aggression against the railway in Truro took place during the evening of 6 August 1942. The raid also turned out to be the most destructive on the city generally. A pair of enemy aircraft strafed the station with machine gun and small cannon fire, killing Mr P. Williams, a railway man, and Mr A.E. Pentecost, a 41-year-old postman-driver who was unfortunately carrying out duties at the station at the time. Some evidence of the raid can still be found in damage to plating on the western side of the passenger footbridge at the west end of the station. A number of other fatal casualties also occurred around the city at the time of the raid on the station, not least of which was the bombing of the infirmary.

Once again wartime resulted in control of the railways being taken over by the Government in the guise of the Railway Executive. Likewise following the end of the war and with the railway companies in a parlous financial state serious consideration was given to nationalisation. The landslide victory of the Labour Party in 1945 brought in a Government committed to the nationalisation of the main public services. And so it was that from 1 January 1948 the Great Western Railway became British Railways (Western Region).

For a number of years the regions simply mirrored the operations of the companies on which their controlling boundaries were largely based and so no great changes took place in the running of the railways in and around Truro. However, in 1951 the controlling arm of British Railways, the British Transport Commission, embarked on the building of a number of classes of standard steam locomotives. Not least among these was the Britannia class, of which ten were initially allocated to depots serving Paddington and the West Country. The first to arrive at Plymouth's (Laira) depot was number 70019 'Lightning'. It was not long before this locomotive and other members of the class were being rostered to take over the down Cornish Riviera and to return with the up working of the express from Penzance the following day.

These locomotives were like nothing else that had ever been seen in Truro and caused great excitement for small boys and big dads. Once again Black Bridge became the grandstand for viewing these striking locomotives. With smoke deflectors, visible outside

Left: *A group of railway workers stop for a picture possibly in the 1930s. Frederick Trebell is probably in there somewhere but it was difficult to tell as this was such a dark little photograph.*

Below: *Frederick Trebell on a day off from the railway with his wife Eliza and her sister Bertha Pascoe and another gentleman, possibly Bertha's husband.*

Great Western Railway

This is to Certify that as the result of the annual examination of the Permanent Way in the Plymouth Division in July 1941. Gang No. 17. Yealmpton Station in which Mr. Frederick Trebell was Lengthman was awarded the Prize for high Standard of Efficiency of Maintenance

Divisional Engineer

Chief Engineer

Left: *This is a copy of a certificate awarded to Frederick Trebell and gang No. 17 in 1941.*

valve gearing, chime whistles and names such as Tornado, Venus, Vulcan and Morning Star, these engines presented a much more modern appearance in contrast to the plain and rather look-alike features of the Great Western engines. Although extremely heavy and powerful, their 4-6-2 wheel arrangement rendered them 'light of foot' and consequently there was much wheel slipping and striving for adhesion before these monsters gathered up their heels and climbed away towards Highertown tunnel with their load of ten or more coaches. Sadly the sight of these splendid locomotives did not last long as they were transferred away to other parts of the country.

In 1955 came the much vaunted British Railways Modernisation Plan. This was to see the almost obscene scrapping of steam locomotives long before their 'sell-by date'. These were to be replaced in the western region by 100 per cent diesel power. On the West of England main line dieselisation was to begin, not as one might suppose in the London area, but in Cornwall.

Hot on the heels of the Modernisation Plan came the appointment of Dr Richard Beeching as Chairman of the British Railways Board; his brief was to eliminate all loss-making aspects of British Rail. These developments combined to bring about radical changes to the railway scene in and about Truro with much shrinkage of railway infrastructure.

The first diesels appeared in 1958 with the short-lived D600 Warship class, the first of which was named Active. Soon, however, it became dubbed Inactive for obvious reasons, much to the delight of enginemen and steam enthusiasts alike. However, the tide of modernisation quickly outpaced the failings of the many early classes of diesels and by early 1963 only a handful of trains remained in the care of steam haulage. The locomotive depot closed to steam in September 1962. The last shedmaster in the days of steam was Mr Joe Stephens who to the very end of his career wore the traditional bowler hat that was so synonymous with that post.

There followed the closure on 6 February 1963 of the Truro to Perranporth and Newquay branch service. On 3 May 1964 the Plymouth Railway Circle and the Railway Correspondence and Travel Society combined to run the official last steam-hauled train to Penzance. Much to the chagrin of Great Western enthusiasts the train was placed in the hands of an immaculately turned out ex Southern Railway West Country class locomotive. The train called only at Bodmin Road, Truro and Redruth. Large crowds gathered at Truro and once again Black Bridge came into its own as did the station buffet where copious amounts of all kinds of drinks were taken on board on this perfect spring day.

In 1965 came a drastic revision in the main-line train services throughout Cornwall. The hitherto local service between Truro and Penzance was almost completely withdrawn along with a number of longer distance trains. This radical pruning of services no doubt brought about the final demise of the locomotive depot which closed entirely in November of that year.

The next decade saw even more rationalisation with pointwork and goods sidings taken out of use between April and November 1971. Two sidings remained for the benefit of trains serving the businesses of Cornwall Farmers and H. Thomas who were able to receive block train workings of agricultural fertilisers. The railways were now no longer interested in running single wagon loads of freight. Unfortunately the service to Cornwall farmers was short lived.

At much the same time number four platform was reduced to a bay, being accessible only by trains from the west. After a few years the line serving this platform was completely closed to other than the occasional exhibition train. The 1970s probably witnessed the railways of Britain at their lowest ebb. However, the turn of the decade and the 1980s heralded a complete reversal in the provision of main-line passenger services from Truro.

The first high-speed trains (HSTs) arrived in 1979 and throughout the 1980s the scheduled journey time to and from London shrank with each change of the public timetable. In 1979 on a conventional locomotive hauled schedule the Golden Hind service took 5 hours 4 minutes to reach Paddington from Truro whereas in 1990 this stood at 4 hours 11 minutes with the Cornish Riviera taking just one minute longer. Regrettably the Golden Hind now takes 4 hours 17 minutes while the Cornish Riviera has slipped to 4 hours 21 minutes. Nonetheless it should be remembered that the HSTs have been performing for 25 years and continue to remain the fastest diesel trains in the world!

The 1980s saw the abolition of the post of stationmaster at Truro and other Cornish stations. However, in place of the stationmaster came the newly created position of Area Manager Cornwall. Once again Truro was at the forefront with the offices being located in new purpose-built premises erected adjacent to the east end of the former platform four.

The most notable appointment to this office was Mr A.H.J. (Rusty) Eplett. Under his aegis the railways acquired a certain autonomy with the introduction of the Cornish Railways brand. It may have been largely cosmetic but it took on a certain air of independence. Most successful of all was the introduction of the Cornish Railcard providing holders with half-price travel between stations in Cornwall and Plymouth. Still obtainable, it now gives a one-third fare reduction in line with all other railcards.

In 1985 the station booking hall underwent a full-scale modernisation with the opening of a new open-plan travel centre. Regrettably modern-day social behaviour has led to the curtailment of this facility and the erection of counter screens.

The 150th anniversary of incorporation of the Great Western Railway was celebrated in 1985 and for the first time in 21 years main-line steam returned to Truro. The magnificently preserved locomotive Clun Castle worked a special train from Plymouth to Truro on 6 September attracting large crowds at the station where the engine was put on display before returning to Plymouth with its train.

The 1990s saw a further retrenchment of the former marshalling yard with only two full-length sidings remaining. The line to Cornwall Farmers Depot having been taken out of use while the trains of agricultural fertiliser to the depot of H. Thomas ceased to run. Now in the twenty-first century there are no regular or even irregular revenue-earning freight trains in West Cornwall!

With the advent of privatisation went the office of Area Manager and, in place of British Rail, Truro is now served by four different passenger-train operating companies: First Great Western which provides all the services to Paddington, Virgin cross-country, doing just that, and Wessex and Wales & Borders providing all other local and longer-distance services. It must be remarked, however, that compared with the 1965 timetable the current service is a vast improvement. It remains to be seen whether the proposed enlarged Greater Western franchise will have a unifying effect and stop the current trend whereby each company seems to operate independently of each other.

In the meantime Truro station unlike most others in the county has retained a fully staffed booking office open throughout the day and early evening, buffet facilities, waiting rooms and uniformed station staff. It is also home to the Cornwall office of the British Transport Police and can boast having CCTV passenger train information monitors throughout the station.

As for the return to steam, there has been much progress since the visit of Clun Castle in 1985. Steam-hauled special trains are now almost an annual event in the county, Black Bridge remaining as always the best viewing platform of all!

The author gratefully acknowledges the help of the Cornish Studies Library of the Cornwall Centre, Redruth, and the Courtney Library of the Royal Institution of Cornwall, Truro, for facilities and permission to consult contemporary newspaper reports, early Ordnance Survey maps and Cornish census returns.

The railway station in 2001.

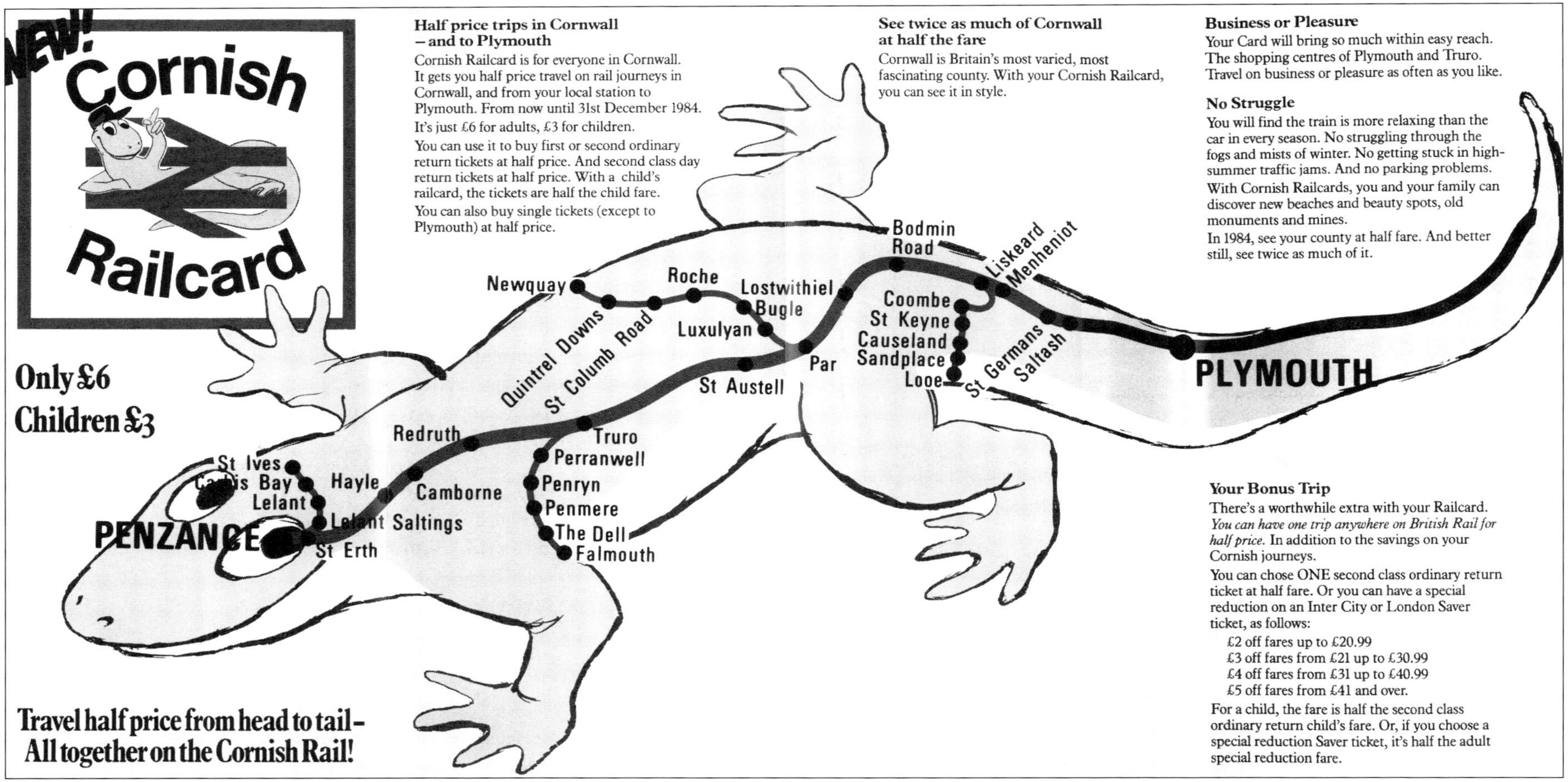

Half price trips in Cornwall – and to Plymouth

Cornish Railcard is for everyone in Cornwall. It gets you half price travel on rail journeys in Cornwall, and from your local station to Plymouth. From now until 31st December 1984.

It's just £6 for adults, £3 for children.

You can use it to buy first or second ordinary return tickets at half price. And second class day return tickets at half price. With a child's railcard, the tickets are half the child fare. You can also buy single tickets (except to Plymouth) at half price.

See twice as much of Cornwall at half the fare

Cornwall is Britain's most varied, most fascinating county. With your Cornish Railcard, you can see it in style.

Business or Pleasure

Your Card will bring so much within easy reach. The shopping centres of Plymouth and Truro. Travel on business or pleasure as often as you like.

No Struggle

You will find the train is more relaxing than the car in every season. No struggling through the fogs and mists of winter. No getting stuck in high-summer traffic jams. And no parking problems. With Cornish Railcards, you and your family can discover new beaches and beauty spots, old monuments and mines.

In 1984, see your county at half fare. And better still, see twice as much of it.

Your Bonus Trip

There's a worthwhile extra with your Railcard. *You can have one trip anywhere on British Rail for half price.* In addition to the savings on your Cornish journeys.

You can chose ONE second class ordinary return ticket at half fare. Or you can have a special reduction on an Inter City or London Saver ticket, as follows:

£2 off fares up to £20.99
£3 off fares from £21 up to £30.99
£4 off fares from £31 up to £40.99
£5 off fares from £41 and over.

For a child, the fare is half the second class ordinary return child's fare. Or, if you choose a special reduction Saver ticket, it's half the adult special reduction fare.

New! Cornish Railcard

Only £6
Children £3

Travel half price from head to tail – All together on the Cornish Rail!

PLYMOUTH

Liskeard
Menheniot
St Germans
Saltash

Bodmin Road
Coombe
St Keyne
Causeland
Sandplace
Looe

Lostwithiel
Bugle
Par

Roche
Luxulyan
St Austell

Quintrel Downs
St Columb Road

Newquay

Truro
Perranwell
Penryn
Penmere
The Dell
Falmouth

Redruth
Camborne
Gwinear Road
Lelant Saltings

St Ives
Carbis Bay
Lelant
St Erth

PENZANCE

A 1984 brochure advertising the new Cornish Railcard.

Chapter 15

✤

Churches, Chapel & Cathedral

A sketch from an old photograph of St Mary's Church. The south aisle still remains and the top of the spire is preserved up at Kenwyn.

Over the years there have been many different religious sects practising their own brand of religion in Truro but it would be a mammoth task to try to include them all.

The Anglican faith had a hard time in Cornwall as the Wesley brothers had made such an impression on the Cornish. John Wesley (1703–91) was always a welcome visitor to Cornwall and often his brother Charles (1707–88) would come with him. Their kind of religion appealed to many of the hard-working locals – farmers, miners and labourers – who had little reward for their work. Often the hope of a reward to come in an afterlife was the most they could wish for. John and Charles came to Truro many times; 1789 was the last visit made by John, but the fervour people felt for his Methodism lasted long after his death.

In 1877 when Queen Victoria ordained and declared 'that the borough of Truro, in the county of Cornwall, shall be a city, and shall be called and styled, 'the City of Truro, in the county of Cornwall,' it meant changes for the Church of England in Truro. The fact that a cathedral was to be built gave a fillip to the Anglicans who were somewhat outnumbered by other denominations. The site of the Parish Church of St Mary was chosen as the place where the new cathedral was to be built. First consecrated in 1259 by Bishop Bronescombe of Exeter, the Parish Church and the Georgian Rectory were to be demolished to make way for the new building, but although the first new bishop, Bishop Benson, was against the 'tinkering up of rotten stones', the decision was made to retain the south aisle of the church and incorporate it into the new building and to this day the south aisle is used as the Parish Church for Truro. At the moment, the cathedral is in need of renovation as much of the stonework on the outside has weathered so badly that the statues are unrecognisable and the decorations in the soft sandstone have worn away. A Chief Executive has been appointed to try to raise the necessary funding. Not only is the building in need of repair but there is also a move afoot to join the diocese of Truro with that of Exeter once more and call the resulting diocese Devonwall!

This move is unlikely to meet with local approval. The Anglicans were not in total decline before the granting of city status and the building of a cathedral. As many as three new churches had been built in Truro in the nineteenth century. St John's Church in Lemon Street was a Philip Sambell designed building and was begun in 1827. St. Paul's Church was built as a chapel of ease to St Clement in 1844 (although the present church is an 1883 building). Both these churches became parishes in their own right in 1865. The third church built at this time was St George's. It was made a parish in 1845 but had to manage without a permanent building for ten years so the services were held in a wooden structure in Back Lane, now City Road.

The first tower of the cathedral to be completed was the clock tower, coated in Cornish copper which of course soon turned green. The clock can be seen projecting from the left-hand side of the tower, an unusual feature as it is rarely seen in photographs having been taken away when it became dangerous. The main tower of the cathedral, the Victoria tower, is under construction so the date should be c.1901 which was when Mr Hawke Dennis gave the money to build the tower in memory of Queen Victoria who had died that year.

Looking from Trelander across the city gives an unusual view of the cathedral looking down on the east window. The law courts, likened to an 'ice-cream sundae' when they were first built, are on the right with the viaduct spanning the valley between the court and the cathedral.

St John's Church is one of Truro's more unusual designs with a dome rather than a tower or steeple.

Truro Methodist Church was built in 1829 in Pydar Street and was another of Philip Sambell's buildings. St George's Methodist Church in St George's Road was designed by Walter Chalmers Smith (1824–1908). Of course Truro has other denominations too, Baptists and Salvation Army both still surviving, and Bible Christians who joined the Methodists in 1907. At one time there was a Primitive Methodist Church in Truro and there was also a sect known as The Shouters. Two sisters, the Misses Downes, were pious ladies who attended the church of the Brianites (later Bible Christians) but during the services they used to shout and scream which upset the other worshippers so they were asked to leave the church. They built their own chapel at the top of Campfield Hill but on the death of one of the sisters the sect died out.

In 1825 Elizabeth Fry the Quaker visited Truro to attend the opening of the Society of Friends new meeting house. The house was built in the corner of the garden of Truro Vean, the home of Mr and Mrs Tweedy. Mr Tweedy had come to Truro to take charge of the Cornish Bank and left a lasting legacy in the form of the Society of Friends Meeting House which is still in use today.

During the Second World War St George's Methodist Church was used during the week as a school for evacuees. It is not known which school used it but it was possibly one from Plymouth, perhaps Stoke Damerel. There was some rivalry between evacuees and the regular churchgoers and youth club. The evacuees brought a cabinet-style gramophone with them and just one record – 'Land of Hope and Glory'. The local youth club knew they

St George's Church with what used to be the Rectory beside it – this is now known as St George's Hotel. The Rectory is now the next house up the road.

were not supposed to touch anything belonging to the evacuees but could not resist playing the record over and over again. Perhaps, however repetitive, it made a nice change to the out-of-tune piano that lived in that room.

In 1949–50 my mother decided that I would attend Sunday School at St George's Methodist and took me one Sunday afternoon and handed me over to the teacher, her friend Frances Hender. All was well and Frances looked after me but could not save me from the horror that was the Sunday school inspector. Aged two, I could not read and only knew two hymns by heart, 'In Our Dear Lord's Garden' and 'Jesus Wants Me For a Sunbeam' and the hymn being sung was neither of these when the inspector walked in. He looked at me and pointed and said in what seemed to be a loud booming voice, 'There is a little girl not singing.' Needless to say I was terrified and shamed to be shown up. I said nothing to my mother when she collected me but the following week I grabbed the railings outside the chapel and refused to go in even though Frances came out and said she would take me in. In desperation my mother walked me over to my grandmother in Kenwyn Street and said, 'I don't know what to do with her mother.' Granny Mitchell thought for a moment, with a china cup of tea part

way to her mouth (there was always a pot of tea on the go at her house as with seven sons and their families there was always someone dropping in), then she said, 'If she won't go to chapel, send her to church.' So for the next 19 years until my work took me away from Truro, I happily attended St Paul's. St George's Methodist is closed for worship now and is home to another establishment, a pre-school group.

H. Miles Brown was the vicar at St Paul's for many years and he always attended the church outings. On one occasion the trip was to a seaside town (possibly somewhere like Polzeath) and after a day on the beach and browsing in the local gift shops most of the congregation settled for a cream tea before returning to the coach for the homeward journey. Although it seems tame now he caused much merriment by querying whether he should put his jam or his cream on to his splits first. He decided to go with the majority and put the jam on first so that he could put the cream elegantly on top but confessed that his inclination was to put the cream first to seal up any holes in the split so that the jam did not drip through!

Paul Vage remembered a story about Guillaume Ormonde, the cathedral organist who was well known for being very forgetful. One day he was

Kenwyn Church and the lych-gate with the schoolroom above. This photo was taken in 2004 and thankfully the scene has not changed for many years. It was because Kenwyn Church was an uphill walk out of the town that St Mary's was built in the centre of Truro.

St Paul's Church at the bottom of Agar Road used to have a Church of England infants school next door. Just visible through the trees, these days that building is a residential home for the elderly.

The cathedral before work started on the two western towers. Posted in Helston in 1905, the card came from a lady called Ada who was writing to her friend who had gone to stay in St Issey and suggested that she 'give Joe your address, I daresay you would like to have a letter from him' and adding as a postscript, 'No offence I hope dear'.

walking up Lemon Street when he met the then dean of the cathedral, Dean Lloyd, coming down. They stopped for a chat, then eventually decided that they must be on their way. Mr Ormonde thought for a moment then said. 'Tell me Dean, when we met was I going up Lemon Street or coming down?' 'You were coming up,' replied the Dean. 'Oh well in that case I haven't had my lunch yet,' said Mr Ormonde, and with that he carried on up the hill.

The Roman Catholic Church in Truro was so bad that in 1884 Father John Grainger bought land in Dereham Terrace and built a church himself. This served the Roman Catholics as the Church of St Piran for many years until in 1972 the church of Our Lady of the Portal and St Piran was built in St Austell Street.

Joyce Teague has a recollection of Sundays when her family lived in Chapel Hill. They attended the Baptist Chapel and each child in her family was given one penny for the collection. As it happened there was an elderly lady living farther up Chapel Hill who made sweets. This poor lady had badly ulcerated legs but this did not put the Teague children off and each week they went up to buy what they called 'billymugs' from this lady. As the billymugs were a halfpenny each, by the time the children got to chapel they each had just one halfpenny to put in the collection. Joyce said that she felt a bit guilty singing 'hear the pennies fall' as the collection was taken as she knew she had spent half of hers on sweets.

St Clement Church in 1988. As this was one of Truro's two original churches, St Paul's later catered for many of the parishioners of St Clement to save them the long walk down to the hamlet.

Chapter 16

✤

St Clement

The path by the river at St Clement c.1900; it is still the same today.

The information in this chapter has been provided by Robert Moor and his sister Margaret Arnall.

St Clement was mentioned in the Domesday Book and still thrives today. It is an attractive hamlet on the bank of the river and those who live there find it a close-knit and friendly community. It is a popular place for families to take a stroll beside the water, or to simply sit and enjoy the peaceful scene, calm water, wooded banks and attractive cottages, some with thatched roofs clustered around the thirteenth-century church. Set in the old manor of Moresk, the church was probably built on the site of an already existing chapel possibly founded and endowed by the Earls of Cornwall who hailed from Condurro before the Conquest.

Through the eyes of an enthusiastic amateur photographer we are given a fascinating glimpse of life in the village from roughly 1880–1910. Interestingly this is the same time-span as the laying of the foundation-stone to the completion of the cathedral. It was a family from Suffolk, whose sons usually went into the Army or the law and who came to settle in St Clement, who provide us with the following information about their family life. Canon Allan Page Moor was a friend of Bishop Benson and

Mrs Eliza Harriet Moor, the vicar's wife.

came to Cornwall to become the vicar of St Clement in 1860, having previously been in Canterbury. His great-grandson Robert tells us that the living of St Clement was in the gift of the Lord Chancellor but it was taken before the Privy Council and the gift of the living was granted to the cathedral. In effect it was swapped for Manaccan. The canon had been at college with Edward White Benson and was pleased to be able to come to this part of the world where he became the librarian for the diocese.

When he arrived in St Clement he and his wife (who was 20 years his junior) had five children and

Above: *Ursula (later Mrs Purefoy) in the Vicarage garden. She was very fond of romantic poses!*

Left: *A family picnic by the river just below the house. Cecilia is the lady kneeling and the young boy may possibly have been a servant, other photographs show the young servant boys in livery.*

altogether his household consisted of 15 people. Because of this they extended and largely rebuilt the Vicarage out of their own funds. The family joke is that the extension was built for three talkative daughters to give the rest of the household some peace and quiet! By 1880 they were having Penmoor built. There was later an argument about the drive to the house and right of access and letters still exist from Robert's great-grandmother Eliza Harriet Moor who obviously felt that having virtually rebuilt the Vicarage it was unfair to try to deny them a driveway to the new house. She was a strong character and was, amongst other things, a founder member of the poor house at St Clement which much later was developed into the isolation hospital. Closer to home, almost on her own doorstep, was River House, bought by them to serve as an orphanage. It was run mainly as a laundry and the well-to-do ladies of the village, as part of their charitable work, drew up a schedule of the tasks that the orphans should perform. It is interesting to note that the lady in charge had a salary of £5 which later rose to £6. Thankfully, while the orphans were attending to their laundry, the vicar's children were out and about taking photographs of everyday scenes.

River House was bought as an orphanage where, amongst other things, the orphans could be trained in laundry work.

Penmoor at St Clement was built in 1880. The builders make an interesting totem pole as they pose for the camera.

The ones shown here were developed from glass plates many years ago by John Allam who later became photographic officer for Cornwall County Fire Brigade. These photos form a small selection of those he developed at the request of Robert's mother, Mrs Moor, about 40 years ago. The vicar's children were Cressica (grandfather of Robert and Margaret), who became an analytical chemist, and Hatherley, who was killed in his early twenties at Ladysmith during the Boer War. He was a major in the artillery regiment and it is his canoe which is seen in several photographs and which the family still own today. The daughters were Cecilia, Margaret and Ursula.

Robert related a story that his father used to tell him; when father was a youngster he used to spend time with his grandparents and was obliged to wear very formal starchy clothes that he hated. He said that the family did not visit Truro often, perhaps twice a week, but when they did they went into town in the coach, a Victoria. On the way back to St Clement anyone 'not important' had to get out of the carriage and walk up St Clement's Hill to ease the burden on the horses. Unfortunately Mr Hunkin, a fervent Christian prone to raising his arms with a 'hallelujah' or falling on his knees before people and praising the Lord, would lie in wait for travellers. The young boy found it embarrassing and the coachman, Peters, apparently found it irritating, as all the way up the hill, Mr Hunkin would be trying to force his form of Christianity on them. Peters' ears would get redder and redder as he got crosser but being a good servant he said nothing. All concerned heaved a sigh of relief as they turned right at the top of the hill and left Mr Hunkin behind. However, his fervent Christianity did rub off on someone as his son later became a much loved Bishop of Truro.

Mr Hunkin was wasting his time preaching to the vicar and his family who were already good Christian souls. Another thing Canon Moor did was to build not only the hall at Malpas as a reading room but also the mission church.

The house as it was several years later with a mature garden.

Margaret in the canoe which the family still have.

The sitting-room at Penmoor.

Ursula in another of her fanciful poses.

The Vicarage c.1880 with the extension on the right which the family jokingly say was added for the three talkative daughters.

Here we see four children by the gate to the well. As this gate was very near the Ship Inn, it is believed that the two girls standing could well be the children of the last landlord, Thomas Andrew, Evelyn and Ann Bath.

Although Margaret Arnall (who helped with information about these photographs) married an Australian, his roots are also at St Clement. His grandfather George Stoughton Arnall was a boat builder at Sunny Corner and no doubt a good one; Mr Arnall came upon a reference to a ship built by his grandfather and launched by his grandmother. The ship concerned was the *Galatea*, but sadly it sank on its maiden voyage.

Another person who fondly remembers growing up in St Clement is Miss Patricia O'Flynn whose father was the vicar there from 1922–32. Together with her brother and sister (they were triplets) she spent very happy years in the village. She quite clearly remembers the time the chimney caught fire and the local boys got together with buckets of water and put out the blaze. The house had two Cornish ranges for cooking, probably harking back to the days when the Moors had such a large household to cater for. The trouble with ranges was that they needed a lot of work to keep them looking nice so no doubt some poor scullery girl had to keep them black leaded. One of the more unpleasant things was that there were rats running around which was not unexpected being so close to the river. With no electricity the oil-lamps were all kept in readiness in the lamp room which was to the left of the front door. Another room which is remembered by Miss O'Flynn and dignified by a name was the 'operation room' where her appendix was removed.

Much later some other residents on the waterfront were Guy Sanders and his wife Helena. They were both very fond of Italy and on one occasion they arrived home from a holiday there complete with a gondola which was a regular sight on the river for many years. When they no longer needed the gondola it was donated to the maritime museum in Exeter. Mrs Sanders was a great cat lover and did much to further their welfare, especially in Italy where there were (and still are) many homeless cats in need of help. In *The Cat* (the magazine of the society, Cats Protection), January/February edition 2003, she is mentioned in an article about the cats in Venice. It was because of her concern about the numbers of unwanted cats and the fact that she started trapping them for a neutering campaign that a society to help stray cats with the unusual name of DINGO was founded; they still continue her work today. The article notes that she was made a Knight of St Mark and the honour was bestowed by Doge Marthoni, so in 1985 she became a Cavaliere di San Marco. It was not only the cats in Venice that concerned her, she also did what she could to help the cats of Florence and when the River Arno flooded she was there to help. Her husband Guy commissioned a piece of wrought-iron work from Byryn Mitchell, the blacksmith in Kenwyn Street, which was placed in Florence at the highest point that the flood had reached. Several years later Byryn and Margaret Mitchell were in Florence and visited the site.

Canon A.P. Moor watches Margaret in her canoe as she paddles alongside the village men with their timber boat.

Possibly a house-guest or a cousin at Penmoor.

Ursula manoeuvres the boat with help from a young boy from the village.

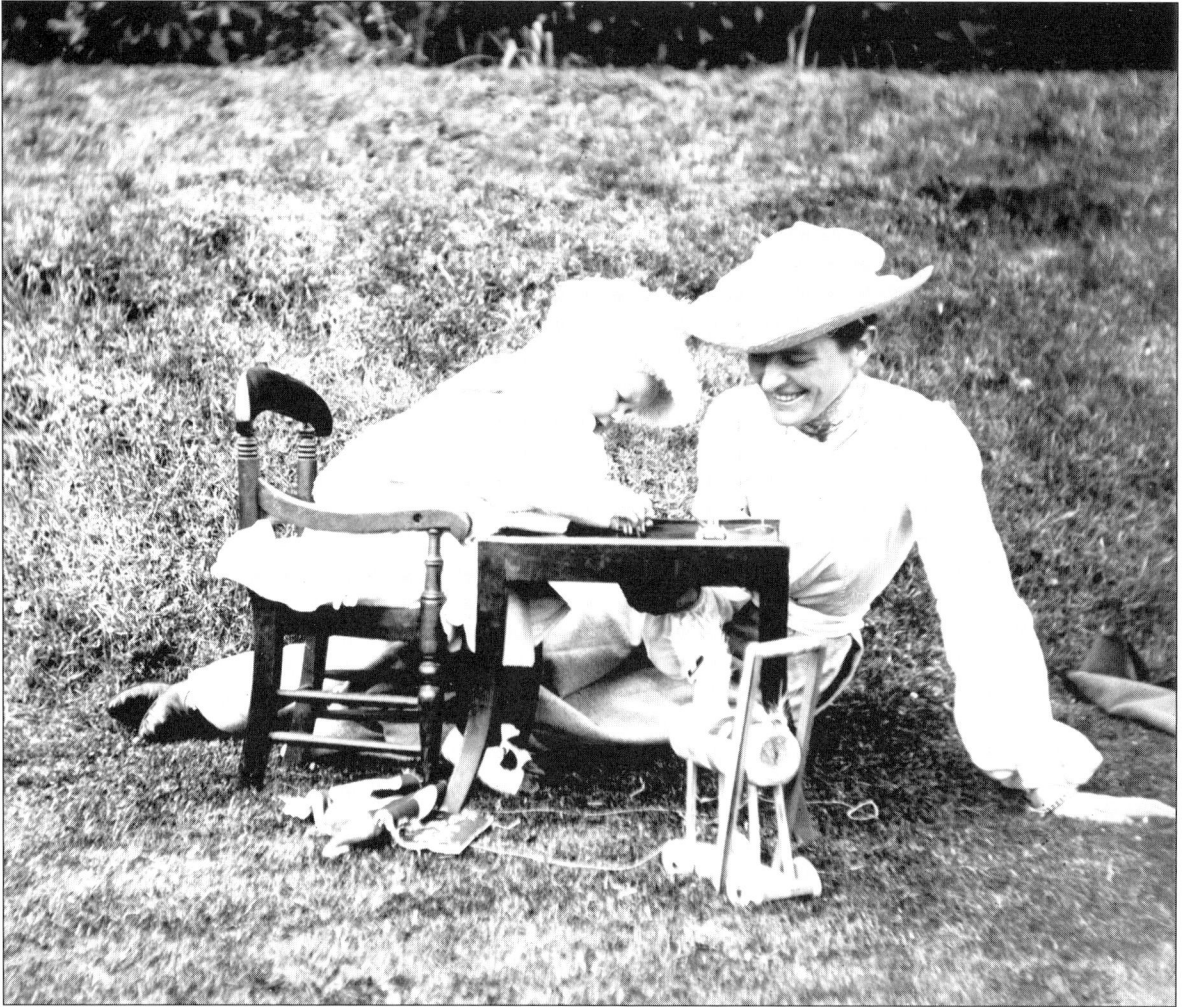

Cecilia who married the consul of Morocco. Her son Cecil Maddern later became the first head of the BBC.

The Moorish servant at Penmoor in 1905.

Two village children stand near the gate to the well which served the hamlet before they had a village pump.

The family pets. The cat and the monkey make an interesting pair. The monkey belonged to Hatherley, the apple of his father's eye who was killed at Ladysmith.

On the back of this photo Guy Sanders has written, 'This is a photograph of my sculpture as it was mounted in Florence (Italy). The pillars and the bracket (which shows the height to which the premises were flooded) were both made by Mitchell the smiths.' The premises to which he refers is a very old company which makes vestments with beautiful silks and another speciality of theirs are the tassels for the vestments. When Byryn and Margaret Mitchell visited the company a few years later with a letter of introduction from 'mister' as they used to call Guy, they were given a tassel as a souvenir of their visit.

This sculpture was made by Guy Sanders to decorate the outside of his house and the pieces of ironwork were made by Byryn Mitchell.

Bibliography

Burley, W.J., *City of Truro 1877–1977*

Truro Buildings and Research Group, 'Pydar Street and the High Cross Area' and 'River Street and its Neighbourhood'

Rowe, Ashley, 'Some Chapters in the History of Truro', in the *West Briton*, c.1930

Parnell, Christine, *Truro: A History and Guide* (Tempus)

Woodfin, R.J., *The Cornwall Railway* (Bradford Barton)

Bennett, Alan, *The Great Western Railway in Mid Cornwall* (Kingfisher Railway Productions)

It looks as if the soldier on the war memorial has been saluting the Victoria tower and the clock tower for the last 82 years!

Subscribers

Mrs J.C. Adams, Truro, Cornwall
Mrs S. Alder, Australia
Doreen and Dennis Barnicoat
Ted and Yvonne Barton, Malpas, Truro
Carol Beaman (née Grose), Truro, Cornwall
David R. Beeston, Cusgarne, Cornwall
Peter and Sheila Blewett, Truro, Cornwall
Vera M. Blewett, Truro, Cornwall
Cedric N. Brown, Chacewater, Truro, Cornwall
Edgar L. Burley, Truro, Cornwall
K.J. Burrow, Bucks Cross, Devon
Paddy and Jane Butler, Truro, Cornwall
Geoff M. Carveth
Barry Champion, Trelissick, Truro
Miss D. Chilcott, Truro, Cornwall
Mrs L.H. Clough, Truro
Simon Coley, St Agnes
June Courage (née Harvey), Truro
Mrs Joan B.L. Craze, Truro, Cornwall
Mrs Rosemary J. Crocker (née Farr)
Andy I.J. Cruickshank
Graham Dash, Truro, Cornwall
Miss Margaret Joy Dash, Truro, Cornwall
Mrs Margaret Dodd, Truro, Cornwall
H. and F. Doughty
R. Jennifer Dunford (née Sheldon), Penryn
Eric Dunn, Keyham, Plymouth
Derek Haydn Endean, Truro, Cornwall
David G. Ferry, Truro, Cornwall
Councillor Miss Constance Fozzard, Mayor 2003–2004
A.T.J. Furse, Quintrell Downs, Newquay
Canon M.B. Geach, Truro, Cornwall
Christopher Goodwyn, Plymouth
Leo C.W. Granville, Truro
Joyce A. Green, Stithians, Truro
Mrs Joan Grose, Truro, Cornwall
Fay Groves, Feock, Truro, Cornwall

Miss Dorothy M. Gundry, Truro
M. Ann Hamlod, Truro, Cornwall
Shaun and Shirley Hamlod, Torquay, Devon
John A. Hancock
Winifred A. Harman, Truro
Cecil Harris, Truro, Cornwall
Peter G.R. Hewson, Truro, Cornwall
Margaret M. Hick, Truro, Cornwall
Christine, Karen and Antony Hill, Truro, Cornwall
Marlene Hill, Truro, Cornwall
Margaret Hocking, Truro, Cornwall
J.A. Hodge
Peter and Gwen Hoggett, Devoran, Cornwall
Lawrence and Chris Holmes, Malpas, Truro, Cornwall
Gerald and Rose Hosken, Goonhavern, Truro, Cornwall
Ruth A. Hoyes (née Cowling), Truro, Cornwall
Janet and James-Carol Ivey, Truro
Anne M. Jacobs
Margaret M. Jennings, Truro, Cornwall
Stella H. Jones, Truro, Cornwall
Susan Kendall, Castle Hill, Truro
Mrs Patricia D. Kinley, Truro, Cornwall
Mrs Elizabeth Lanxon
Anne Lean, Truro, Cornwall
Mrs Elizabeth E. Libby, Truro, Cornwall
Susan A. Lyndon
Arthur Lyne
John MacCoughlan, Truro, Cornwall
Mrs Barbara Martin, Frogpool, Chacewater, Truro, Cornwall
Barbara and Brian May, Truro, Cornwall
Mr David J. and Mrs Betty May, Truro, Cornwall
Harry M. May, Grampound Road, Truro

Lesley May, Rustington, Sussex
Spencer May, Sydney, Australia
Malcolm McCarthy, Padstow
Christine E. McWalters (née Verran), Truro, Cornwall
Peter Messer-Bennetts, Portscatho
Harvey Joseph Wallace Mitchell, Truro, Cornwall
Marlene H. Mitchell
Michele Morris, Goring-By-Sea, Sussex
Ernestine Nicholls, Truro, Cornwall
Patricia S. O'Flynn, Truro, Cornwall
Barbara Olds, Truro, Cornwall
Mr Fred B. Paddy, Truro, Cornwall
Neville H. Paddy
Mr Tony Paddy, Kidlington, Oxford
David S. Palmer, Osokosie, Truro, Cornwall
Bernard J. Pearce, Truro, Cornwall
Mrs Eileen Penhale, Easebourne, Midhurst, West Sussex
Jeffrey G. Penhaligon, Truro, Cornwall
Malcolm Penrose, Truro, Cornwall
Margaret E. Perry, Truro, Cornwall
John Pollock, Perranwell, Truro
Barbara Ann Pooley, Truro
Peter F. Portwood, Truro
Des and Elaine Prouse, Truro, Cornwall
Roger Reay
Linda Rix, Come-To-Good, Truro
Mrs Mary Roberts, Truro

William M. Roberts, Truro
Mike and Sharman Rowe, Truro, Cornwall
Jeffrey J. Rumble, St Feock, Truro, Cornwall
Trevor Scoble (Junior), Truro, Cornwall
Ken Searle, Pool, Redruth
Marjorie Shaw, Tresillian, Truro
Peter B. Sheldon, Truro
Denis R. Sloman, Truro, Cornwall
Diana Smith, Truro, Cornwall
John W. Steele, Truro, Cornwall
Gregory S. Stephens, Truro
Ray Stephens, Tresillian, Cornwall
R.G. Teague, Truro, Kernow
Barrie and Sue Thomas, Devoran, Cornwall
Elwyn Thomas, Auctioneer
Mr Terry Thomas, Truro, Cornwall
A. Orchid Tonkin, Truro, Cornwall
Harold T. Tonkin
Julia A. Tregaskis, Truro, Cornwall
Mavis Trounce, Portloe, Truro, Cornwall
Mr Rodney J. Verran
Amy and Katy Vincent, Truro, Cornwall
John F.W. Walling, Newton Abbot, Devon
Colin and Wendy Ward, Probus, Cornwall
Rodney O. Warmington, Truro
F. John Warne, Tregony, Cornwall
Canon M. and Mrs R. Warner
C.N. Wiblin, Shrewton, Wiltshire
Margaret Willis, Truro
D.C. Woolcock

Community Histories

The Book of Addiscombe • Canning and Clyde Road Residents Association and Friends
The Book of Addiscombe, Vol. II • Canning and Clyde Road Residents Association and Friends
The Book of Axminster with Kilmington • Les Berry and Gerald Gosling
The Book of Bampton • Caroline Seward
The Book of Barnstaple • Avril Stone
The Book of Barnstaple, Vol. II • Avril Stone
The Book of The Bedwyns • Bedwyn History Society
The Book of Bickington • Stuart Hands
Blandford Forum: A Millennium Portrait • Blandford Forum Town Council
The Book of Bramford • Bramford Local History Group
The Book of Breage & Germoe • Stephen Polglase
The Book of Bridestowe • D. Richard Cann
The Book of Bridport • Rodney Legg
The Book of Brixham • Frank Pearce
The Book of Buckfastleigh • Sandra Coleman
The Book of Buckland Monachorum & Yelverton • Pauline Hamilton-Leggett
The Book of Carharrack • Carharrack Old Cornwall Society
The Book of Carshalton • Stella Wilks and Gordon Rookledge
The Parish Book of Cerne Abbas • Vivian and Patricia Vale
The Book of Chagford • Iain Rice
The Book of Chapel-en-le-Frith • Mike Smith
The Book of Chittlehamholt with Warkleigh & Satterleigh • Richard Lethbridge
The Book of Chittlehampton • Various
The Book of Colney Heath • Bryan Lilley
The Book of Constantine • Moore and Trethowan
The Book of Cornwood and Lutton • Compiled by the People of the Parish
The Book of Creech St Michael • June Small
The Book of Cullompton • Compiled by the People of the Parish
The Book of Dawlish • Frank Pearce
The Book of Dulverton, Brushford, Bury & Exebridge • Dulverton and District Civic Society
The Book of Dunster • Hilary Binding
The Book of Edale • Gordon Miller
The Ellacombe Book • Sydney R. Langmead
The Book of Exmouth • W.H. Pascoe
The Book of Grampound with Creed • Bane and Oliver
The Book of Hayling Island & Langstone • Peter Rogers
The Book of Helston • Jenkin with Carter
The Book of Hemyock • Clist and Dracott
The Book of Herne Hill • Patricia Jenkyns
The Book of Hethersett • Hethersett Society Research Group
The Book of High Bickington • Avril Stone
The Book of Ilsington • Dick Wills
The Book of Kingskerswell • Carsewella Local History Group
The Book of Lamerton • Ann Cole and Friends
Lanner, A Cornish Mining Parish • Sharron Schwartz and Roger Parker
The Book of Leigh & Bransford • Malcolm Scott
The Book of Litcham with Lexham & Mileham • Litcham Historical and Amenity Society
The Book of Loddiswell • Loddiswell Parish History Group
The New Book of Lostwithiel • Barbara Fraser
The Book of Lulworth • Rodney Legg
The Book of Lustleigh • Joe Crowdy

The Book of Lyme Regis • Rodney Legg
The Book of Manaton • Compiled by the People of the Parish
The Book of Markyate • Markyate Local History Society
The Book of Mawnan • Mawnan Local History Group
The Book of Meavy • Pauline Hemery
The Book of Minehead with Alcombe • Binding and Stevens
The Book of Morchard Bishop • Jeff Kingaby
The Book of Newdigate • John Callcut
The Book of Nidderdale • Nidderdale Museum Society
The Book of Northlew with Ashbury • Northlew History Group
The Book of North Newton • J.C. and K.C. Robins
The Book of North Tawton • Baker, Hoare and Shields
The Book of Nynehead • Nynehead & District History Society
The Book of Okehampton • Roy and Ursula Radford
The Book of Paignton • Frank Pearce
The Book of Penge, Anerley & Crystal Palace • Peter Abbott
The Book of Peter Tavy with Cudlipptown • Peter Tavy Heritage Group
The Book of Pimperne • Jean Coull
The Book of Plymtree • Tony Eames
The Book of Porlock • Dennis Corner
Postbridge – The Heart of Dartmoor • Reg Bellamy
The Book of Priddy • Albert Thompson
The Book of Princetown • Dr Gardner-Thorpe
The Book of Rattery • By the People of the Parish
The Book of St Day • Joseph Mills and Paul Annear
The Book of Sampford Courtenay with Honeychurch • Stephanie Pouya
The Book of Sculthorpe • Gary Windeler
The Book of Seaton • Ted Gosling
The Book of Sidmouth • Ted Gosling and Sheila Luxton
The Book of Silverton • Silverton Local History Society
The Book of South Molton • Jonathan Edmunds
The Book of South Stoke with Midford • Edited by Robert Parfitt
South Tawton & South Zeal with Sticklepath • Roy and Ursula Radford
The Book of Sparkwell with Hemerdon & Lee Mill • Pam James
The Book of Staverton • Pete Lavis
The Book of Stithians • Stithians Parish History Group
The Book of Stogumber, Monksilver, Nettlecombe & Elworthy • Maurice and Joyce Chidgey
The Book of Studland • Rodney Legg
The Book of Swanage • Rodney Legg
The Book of Tavistock • Gerry Woodcock
The Book of Thorley • Various
The Book of Torbay • Frank Pearce
The Book of Watchet • Compiled by David Banks
The Book of West Huntspill • By the People of the Parish
Widecombe-in-the-Moor • Stephen Woods
Widecombe – Uncle Tom Cobley & All • Stephen Woods
The Book of Williton • Michael Williams
The Book of Witheridge • Peter and Freda Tout and John Usmar
The Book of Withycombe • Chris Boyles
Woodbury: The Twentieth Century Revisited • Roger Stokes
The Book of Woolmer Green • Compiled by the People of the Parish

For details of any of the above titles or if you are interested in writing your own history, please contact: Commissioning Editor, Community Histories, Halsgrove House, Lower Moor Way, Tiverton Business Park, Tiverton, Devon EX16 6SS, England; email: katyc@halsgrove.com